Banking Through
the
Looking Glass

Banking Through

the

Looking Glass

Based on the Seminar held at
Christ's College, Cambridge, 6–11 September 1987

The Chartered Institute of Bankers

10 Lombard Street, London EC3V 9AS

Chartered Institute of Bankers (CIB) Publications
Published under exclusive licence and royalty agreement by Bankers Books Ltd.

Copies can be obtained from:
THE CHARTERED INSTITUTE OF BANKERS
10 Lombard Street
London
EC3V 9AS

© The Chartered Institute of Bankers or Author, 1987

ISBN 0 85297 202 4

Cartoons by Ben Shailo
Cover design by Nick Zoller

Typeset in 10 pt on 12 pt Baskerville by McCorquodale (Scotland) Ltd.
Text printed on 100 gsm Combat Economy Cartridge. Cover 240 mic Astralux One Sided Card.
Printed and bound by McCorquodale (Scotland) Ltd. for Blades East and Blades Limited.

CONTENTS

ROBERT RENDEL
Director, Cambridge Seminar 1987

FOREWORD

The theme of the sixteenth Cambridge Seminar was that, in facing the challenge of continuous change, we can learn much from the ways in which our markets and our competitors see us.

The "Looking Glass" of the title was held up for us by four eminent observers. Each brought a very different perspective to bear but all recognised that we are in the thick of a period of rapid development for banks and financial services generally—and we shall stay there. It is not a one-off development but rather a major acceleration in a continuing process.

This book is published not only as a permanent record for those present but, more importantly, for those who were not. Its aim is to challenge readers to think. I trust it succeeds.

ROBERT RENDEL
Director, Cambridge Seminar 1987

Derek F. Channon

Derek Channon is Professor of Marketing at Manchester Business School.

He has been actively engaged in research into the strategic management process of financial service organisations worldwide and in the development of the International Banking Centre at MBS since its inception. He has acted as a consultant to a large number of banks and financial service institutions in Europe, North America, Africa and the Far East.

Professor Channon has written extensively on the changing strategies of participants in the financial service industry and also lectured all over the world on bank and financial service industry strategy.

Derek F. Channon

1. THE PERSONAL CUSTOMER'S VIEW

Contents

"I've forgotten my pin number—
could you give me a hint?"

THE PERSONAL CUSTOMER'S VIEW

The changing patterns of retail financial services

This year's seminar is entitled 'Banking Through the Looking Glass' in an effort to consider the banking industry from the point of view of the customer. As the degree of competition within the banking industry has heated up it is pleasant to see a growing recognition that the customer is once again being looked on as the reason for being in business rather than as an interruption to doing business. This paper addresses itself to the market for retail financial services by looking at who the retail customers actually are, examining what services they want, and looking at the ways banks are seeking to provide these services.

The term 'retail financial services' is used, rather than 'banking', to emphasise the breakdown of the traditional demarcation barriers between the historic specialist sectors of the financial services industry. In all sectors, many institutions are presently seeking to penetrate markets traditionally serviced by specialists. Thus banks were the primary suppliers of transmission services, the main recipient of current account deposits, major players in medium-term deposits and, via specialist subsidiaries, the main providers of consumer credit finance and card based services. Building societies became the main recipients of consumer savings deposits and the main supplier of mortgage credit. Insurance companies and brokers were the main suppliers of life and non-life, personal and family risk cover and held a high share of longer term investment savings. Brokerage and investment management companies were the other major providers of investment management services.

Today all these traditional barriers are being broken down as a consequence, in large part, of deregulation and new technology. This is transforming operating cost structures and also providing new, alternative, forms of service delivery which can dramatically change the relative positions of traditional competitors from both within and outside the industry. In addition the changes are causing major shakeouts in all sectors, leading to mergers within sectors, with smaller competitors being absorbed by larger ones or bought by new entrants. Overall, substantially increased concentration is developing within the financial services industry, but within each sector competition is actually increasing as new, powerful entrants compete with the established traditional sector leaders.

Today banks have therefore become major players in housing finance, and are attempting to grow in investment management and insurance. Building societies are pushing to develop their position as full service, retail financial service companies by offering transmission services, card based products, non-mortgage consumer credit, full-time insurance brokerage and investment management services. Insurance companies have also expanded their role as investment managers and are developing their position in mortgage finance.

In addition there are many new entrants to the market. These include entrants from overseas and from other industries. The main automobile companies, for example, have rapidly built up their financial service businesses from traditional bases in auto finance. In particular, many major retailers have seen the potential in providing financial services through existing store locations as a way of encouraging customer loyalty and improving their merchandise offer.

Overall then, we are seeing an industry in a state of very rapid change with the apparent evolution of a series of major players, each trying to provide a comprehensive service to the retail market. It remains to be seen, however, if customers actually *want* to purchase all their financial service needs from one supplier. Indeed, consumer perceptions of what services a bank, for example, provides may not accurately reflect the actual breadth of product range on offer. This results from the bank failing to communicate adequately its range of services to the customer by poor marketing, and a growing trend for customers not to need to visit branches – so avoiding the primary delivery point for the bank to offer its retail financial services.

By contrast, many institutions, rather than trying to provide all services to all people, are actually targeting very precisely the offerings they wish to make to very carefully defined groups of customers. While the large general purpose institutions may similarly wish to address themselves to specific market segments it could well be that offering products alone is not enough and that modifications, in particular in delivery systems, may well be another essential factor in satisfying market segment needs as efficiently and effectively as the niche market specialists.

Who are the customers and what do they want?

While virtually everyone is a candidate for some financial services, different groups need different services in different amounts via different delivery systems. Some individuals will be much more price sensitive than others. Substantial differences also occur in the relative costs and profitability of providing certain services to particular customer groups. Understanding what different groups of consumers need and how they want their financial services provided are therefore critical success factors in modern banking.

Bankers, however, are only just beginning to understand how to subdivide, or segment, markets and to design products and delivery systems which provide efficient, effective service to selected customer groups at an acceptable level of risk and profitability. Ironically, much of the data required to understand how, when, where, why and how much consumers want particular services is contained within the banks' own accounting systems. Regrettably, however, the banks do not yet have in place the integrated data base management systems to interrogate this data, in order to convert the data into information useful for guiding management decisions. Moreover, there are few senior bankers at present who have the strategic marketing skills to interpret such information and then to convert it into a guide to formulate a strategy for the retail market.

Strategic segmentation is thus a critical ingredient in the design of a successful retail banking strategy. How then can the retail market be subdivided into significant groups of customers for whom banks can provide suitable services? Several approaches have been successfully tried and normally a number of segmentation methods are used conjointly to arrive at a specific target group profile.

One simple, but important, device is to divide customers into groups based upon their level of affluence. Using this methodology we can identify a series of groups which a number of the niche strategy institutions have quite specifically targeted. The main such groups are:—

The Very Rich: This group constitutes a small, but very important, group of individuals with investible assets of, say, £1m or more. Such individuals tend to be male, 50 years or more of age, well travelled, moderately financially sophisticated and desirous of a high level of personal service. To meet such needs, private banking specialist units have been created in many banks, usually located in no- or low-tax environments. Individual personal account managers have been appointed to look after the interests of such individuals who will generally tend to conduct their affairs through advisers and a series of specialist institutions, not allowing any one of them to gain a full understanding of their financial service requirements.

The Rich: A considerably larger group with some £100,000 of investible assets; again such individuals tend to be male and over 45. At this level of investible assets, they will again tend to use a variety of specialist providers of financial services. Investment management will therefore tend to be via a brokerage house, again with a personal investment manager. Such individuals, however, require less international servicing. While maintaining one or more bank accounts for transactions and possibly non-mortgage borrowing, they are unlikely to utilise clearing banks for asset management services.

High Net Worth Individuals (HNWIs): Usually deemed to have investible assets of £15,000-£100,000, this group constitutes a semi-mass market. In each developed country a number of institutions have focused on providing services to this critical group. In the UK such a group represents a very small number of building society accounts but a critical component in the movement's deposit base. Merrill Lynch, American Express and Citibank have also all focused on this group worldwide. These individuals tend to be white collar executives, 45+ years of age, married and with medium to high incomes. The companies targeting such accounts have attempted to pick off their investment, insurance and credit requirements, leaving transaction services to conventional banks. The classic product offering to this group, which has attracted over one million customers to Merrill Lynch alone, has been the Cash Management Account which combines the chequing facility of a bank with a credit card, market interest rates on all credit balances and an automatic credit line based on the value of assets under management. Refinements on the original product have increased the number of investment options and permitted the equity value locked up in personal property to be converted to instant liquidity.

Interestingly, the companies mentioned have tended to use direct marketing approaches to reach this customer base: Merrill Lynch via telemarketing, and Amex via direct mail to its card base. Citibank, similarly, used direct mail to its Diners Club card base, but has also segregated its branches in New York to provide a superior, personalised service to account holders with balances of over $25,000.

To date, the major UK clearing banks, by contrast, while expressing their considerable interest in this market group, have actively done little to provide them with special services. Some banks have introduced gold card versions of their credit cards, special high interest deposit accounts, automatic credit lines and the like, but little effort has been made to personalise transaction service delivery, to introduce sweep accounts or products like the Merrill Lynch Cash Management Account or even to market actively to their own existing base of high net worth individuals.

Medium Net Worth Individuals (MNWIs): This group constitutes the largest number of significant savers and represents the bulk of the personal deposit market for both banks and building societies in the UK with average deposit balances of £1,000-£12,000. Such deposits are mainly held by building societies where customers have traditionally been offered superior deposit services to those available from the clearing banks. Although this group also accounts for a relatively small share of the societies' account base, it represents the core of their deposit base. It is also this group which has perhaps become the new purchasers of equities in the UK as the privatisation of nationalised industries has extended share ownership.

This group, too, tends to make use of multiple institutions for their financial services but is the most important target segment for the emerging financial supermarkets. However, since many of these net savers tend to be 45 and over, they may well prove very difficult to convince of the benefits of an integrated financial service package, especially if the present proposed rules on polarisation remain unchanged and banks have to decide to broke competitors' products or sell only their own.

The MNWI group should perhaps be included as a segment within what might loosely be called the "mass market"; however, it can be broken out and has been targeted by a number of institutions. Interestingly perhaps, it is also a sector targeted by some retailers, most notably Marks & Spencer. The bottom of the MNWI segment also tends to represent the level at which banking services delivered via a conventional branch network remains profitable. High borrowers, without deposits, are also profitable, but non-borrowers with low deposits tend to be loss-making due to the way in which transmission services are cross subsidised in the UK by current account balances.

The remainder of the mass retail market can be segmented using conventional market research techniques. Traditionally, these focused upon socio-demographic characteristics but, more recently, these have proved less reliable and today many consumer goods companies prefer to focus on combinations of socio-demographics, family lifecycle and lifestyle.

Socio-demographers divide the population by characteristics such as age, income, job classification, geography and the like. The UK is well served with systems such as ACORN which permit carefully targeted communications to reach specific socio-demographic household segments based on the development of a series of profiles for all the property in urban areas throughout the country.

A refinement to socio-demographic characteristics focuses on family lifecycle position. This indicates the changing purchasing properties of individuals at different stages in their lives. The system can be applied to all types of products and services. For example, young bachelors tend to have few financial burdens, are interested in fashion and leisure activities and, as a consequence, will be active purchasers of vacations, sporty cars, basic furniture and mating game equipment. By contrast, "full nest 1" where the youngest child is still under six is most interested in building the family home, is short of cash and is interested in new, especially advertised, products. Major purchases for this group include domestic appliances, DIY materials, and children's products such as medicines, toys and clothing.

When applied to financial service products it is found that instalment credit products are heavily used by young marrieds and least used by empty nest retired. Mortgage credit tends to be less used by young marrieds and most by full nest families. ATM usage is highest amongst bachelors and young marrieds while time deposits come mainly from empty nest groups and least from bachelors.

Lifestyle segmentation adds yet a further refinement to socio-demographic and lifecycle methods of dividing the mass market. Terms that have become commonplace as descriptors in the UK include YUPPIES, young, upwardly progressing individuals; DINKIES, dual income, no kids individuals; and GLAMS, greying, leisured, affluent marrieds. It is perhaps interesting to note that the latter group, which have tended to be neglected by fashion retailers, banks and the like, actually have today the greatest spending power, the highest need for investment management services, and are a key source of bank and building society deposits.

In the USA a number of alternative lifestyle segments have also been specifically identified with regard to their usage of financial service industry products and services. There, it was found that the market could be divided into five lifestyle groups, namely:–

Givers: This group, which made up 19 per cent of the market, were the individuals who primarily provided the deposit base of financial institutions and took little credit. Such individuals tended to be 40-60 years old, living on medium incomes, had children who had just left home, and had lived in their house for more than 5 years.

Takers: These individuals constituted some 17 per cent of the market and were the main users of non-mortgage credit. They were usually aged below 45, and again enjoyed medium incomes; if married, they often had children at home, and were very likely to have lived in their houses for less than five years.

Rollers: These individuals made up only 4.3 per cent of the market but were both heavy users of credit and had high levels of deposits. Such individuals enjoyed high levels of income, were most likely to have had a university education, had white collar jobs, and were 35-45 years old.

Marginal Players: These individuals constituted the largest group in the market, 38 per cent, and had limited deposits and little credit. Such individuals were profitable to service, but only just. They were mainly under 45, had medium incomes, had blue collar jobs, and large households.

Clutter: The last group, making up 20 per cent of the market, had few deposits and used little or no credit. These individuals usually cost a bank money to service, especially when done through a branch network, as such individuals tended to be high users of transaction services. Such individuals were most likely to be single, have moved house in the past five years, have low incomes, no college education and were under 35 years of age.

Utilising segmentation techniques such as these, it is interesting perhaps to note how Citibank Individual Bank developed its strategy in the New York market. Firstly the bank identified and analysed the cost of providing services to different market segments and their different service usage pattern. As a result, the bank concluded that customers wanted a high level of convenience for transactions but did not require a full range of services at all branches. High net worth individuals did, however, want, and were prepared to pay for, a superior level of service. As a result the bank reduced its branch network from 260 to 220 offices; reduced staff from 7,000 to 5,000; but increased service delivery capacity by introducing more than 500 ATMs located in branch lobbies or at remote sites. Customers with over $25,000 of balances were handled by personal financial advisers in special branches which were pleasantly furnished or alternatively in segregated areas of existing branches. Those with account balances of $3,000 or more could use the conventional teller system but were encouraged by differential pricing to use ATMs for transaction services. Customers with less than $3,000 in balances were separated into five segments with most of the clutter and marginal player types being encouraged to bank elsewhere by weeding out payroll accounts and charging for transaction services. While, for a period, these tactics brought Citibank some bad press, at the end their market share had doubled and profitability had dramatically increased.

Given that it is possible carefully to segment the retail market, how well do the financial service industry concerns in the UK actually do it? How well are the services they provide targeted to meet the needs of particular customer groups? How appropriately do they communicate these services? How suitable is the system of delivering the services to the customers?

What customer segmentation is undertaken?

Financial service institutions have made considerable steps in using segmentation mainly by appealing to specific customer groups at a particular point in time, especially to gain new accounts which it is hoped will be retained and become attractive later in life. For example, banks and building societies have both wooed the children's pocket-money market, attempting to attract small savers to encourage the savings habit amongst the young and to gain accounts for later in life. Whether such an approach is profitable is debatable, despite the extremely low rates of interest paid on such accounts by some banks.

The student market has also been a focal point for all the main clearing banks for many years, on the assumption that capturing accounts at the undergraduate stage will lead to the later development of attractive customers. This may well be true, although it must be said that many students do not emerge as high net worth individuals and a more selective approach to students from professional schools or business schools might yield a better harvest. However, the true value of exploiting the student market should come after graduation when the student initially joins the bachelor group of 'takers', or requires mortgage lending on marriage. Unless follow-up marketing occurs therefore, the losses incurred in obtaining and keeping the account during the university period seem wasted. At present, however, banks do not tend to have such follow-up marketing effort in place.

The Midland and TSB have perhaps been amongst the most innovative in lifestyle targeting, especially to younger customer segments. The Midland campaign positioning of Vector seems clearly aimed at the young working professionals and is an interesting rebundled service account with a fixed charge to cover the cost of transactions. The TSB has been innovative in linking discounts with its services as a means of attracting the youth market.

All these efforts, you will note, seem directed at the two largest groups in the market, namely those identified as marginal players and clutter, where the bank's profitability is lowest or negative. This is the opposite of the Citibank approach. The argument advanced to support such a strategy is that as these accounts mature they will become increasingly attractive. This is, however, only partially true. Many such accounts will remain unattractive and marketing effort devoted to selecting attractive accounts could be an alternative approach to one which assumes that customer inertia will continue to be the key factor in determining where individuals bank.

Credit market segmentation

Segmentation in the credit market tends to be much less specific and directed at purpose of use. A large element of consumer credit is therefore provided by credit finance companies, retailers or card based systems rather than as direct credit lines from banks. Building societies have historically been excluded from this market although some top-up mortgage lending was redirected into consumer durables purchasing. Consumers tend to want finance to be available at the point of purchase of the goods or service they want the money for. As direct providers of such finance, banks can be said to have done a poor job, although their credit finance and card subsidiaries have been much more aggressive. Barclaycard and, more recently, Trustcard, appear to have been most aggressive amongst the card companies with the Access banks being much less so.

Again, however, little use is presently made of the purchasing information available to the card companies to identify specific segments from amongst the card user files. For example, it is possible to interrogate such a card file to observe which individuals use their cards for travel, entertainment, household purchases, motoring and the like and, via the monthly statements, to offer supplementary products or services of particular interest to individuals rather than offers of cheap bric-a-brac from direct mail companies. Similarly, credit finance companies tend to build their books by direct marketing to the retail trade rather than the ultimate consumer. Such pinpoint marketing to the consumer is, however, being actively exploited by retailers who have been steadily building their own card base, offering extensive lines of credit, encouraging credit roll over by additional purchases, and taking the margin previously enjoyed by the bank card and credit finance companies.

Recently a number of financial institutions have been actively soliciting customers, notably homeowners, via direct marketing, to take medium-term loans to pay off other credit lines such as hire purchase, store cards and credit cards, and offering rates between overdraft lines and the extremely high rates of interest paid for card-based credit. Whether these will be very successful is unclear since in practice many consumers tend not to be interest rate sensitive in their purchase of items on credit, although they are very sensitive to the size of the actual monthly repayment. Moreover, most consumers do not aggregate their payments in this way, but rather recognise that they pay so much per month to each institution with whom they have a credit facility.

Until recently the largest single area of personal credit, mortgage finance, was hardly segmented at all except for first time buyers and the market for very large mortgages. It was a sellers' market and innovation was limited. More recently, the market has become extremely competitive with many new entrants, including the banks and insurance companies. Innovations have also occurred in financing, even including the development of securitised mortgages. The mortgagee has also become recognised as a particularly attractive potential customer for a series of additional financial services, including conveyancing, real estate brokerage, property insurance, personal life, investment services and the like. As a consequence, and with the deregulation of the building society movement, a dramatic transformation is taking place, not only in the supply of finance, but also in the delivery systems for this and peripheral products. Many of the leading building societies have actively begun to enter the market for real estate brokerage by acquisition or adding such services to their existing networks, and by adding terminal driven full line insurance broking and conveyancing services. They have also been joined by some banks and insurance companies, such that the real estate brokerage industry which was traditionally highly fragmented has, in the space of about four years, become quite concentrated.

Little real segmentation of mortgagees has, however, yet developed. In part, this has been because building societies traditionally did not keep information on these critical customers. Unlike banks, which carefully monitored their borrowers to keep credit risks under control, building societies had such low loan loss rates that, provided a borrower was in good standing, there was no reason to contact him because the societies were restricted from offering other financial services. The main objective of the societies themselves, moreover, was not to make profits, since they were mutual organisations, but to spread home ownership to as many as possible.

Investment market segmentation

Despite the fact that 'givers' and 'rollers' are among the most easily identified segments, most financial service corporations have made little effort to appeal specifically to lifecycle or lifestyle segments in the market for investment funds. Even amongst HNWIs, for example, who might be holders of gold cards, the card companies offer automatic credit lines rather than attempt to market investment management services. Further, in most banks little effort is made to attract or retain significant depositors. In addition, although building societies have attempted to reduce their book mismatch by offering better terms for longer deposits, little active marketing is then undertaken to the existing depositor-base to encourage funds retention. Here it is assumed that term deposits are a form of savings and compete with other forms of investments such as unit trusts, equities and whole life funds. The main consumer marketing message by all forms of institution thus tends to stress rates of interest or profit performance rather than being targeted at the specific future needs of individuals. It is aimed at stimulating immediate purchase instead of generating loyalty or account retention.

This position may change with the encouragement of personal transportable pension plans, the development of PEPs and the broadening of the ownership base for equities. Banks, in particular, have been weak in offering attractive deposit products, although they have been more active in building up their investment management interests. The recent purchase by the TSB of Target is such an example. There are signs, however, that money market interest rates on all deposit balances, including current accounts, will become normal before long, especially as the leading building societies step up their marketing of transaction services. As a consequence, there will be a gradual move away from the integration of deposit and transaction services

By contrast, in the United States there have been significant moves to segment the investment market using a variety of approaches including nationwide telemarketing to solicit for deposits; the development of personal investment counsellors covering a portfolio of service offerings; active soliciting by brokerage houses of different segments of the mass market for investors, such as professional women, those about to retire and the like; targeted direct mail marketing; and the design of specific products or services to appeal to particular customer groups. Substantial refinements in the approach of many UK organisations are therefore likely when the full potential of profitability from investment management opportunities are better recognised.

Delivery system development

While it can be argued that the banks and building societies have not necessarily catered well for specific target group customer needs in credit and investment services, they have dramatically improved the options open to individuals in transaction services by offering a growing variety of mechanisms for performing them. Whereas the majority of transactions in the UK are still cash based, non cash methods are now much more varied than the traditional cheque. Today consumers can use debit and credit cards, ATMs, telephone banking, home banking and will shortly have EFTPOS.

While many of the new electronic transaction systems have been introduced to help reduce the cost for the banks of paper based systems, rather than to provide extra convenience to consumers, they have brought about another major side effect which was not intended. Notably they transfer to the customer the option to choose the time, the place and the method of undertaking the transaction. As a consequence, there is no particular need for the customers to go into the branches of the banks – the most expensive components in the banks' cost structure and the present primary delivery system for the array of products and services they wish to sell to consumers. Moreover, as telephone banking and home banking expand and ATMs perhaps develop into smart terminals, the number of delivery points controlled by customers will dramatically exceed in number those controlled by the financial institutions. The original source of power of the banks – control over the transaction and transmission systems – thus potentially becomes reduced to that of being operators of a computer switching system.

At the present moment this scenario is not unrealistic when taken from the customer's point of view. The last place in the British high street that people like to enter is, apparently, the traditional men's tailoring store. The next least favourite place to visit is a branch of a clearing bank. Why should this be? Consider the traditional make up of the design of a branch. It consists of a limited floor area given over to customer services, while the bulk is devoted to back office operations. Only the simplest paying in and out transactions are handled by the tellers, who are the customers' main interface with the bank, and anything out of the ordinary must be customer initiated at a separate window, which is not even permanently manned. If a customer wants any sort of service such as a loan, an insurance policy, investment advice or the like, he or she has firstly to ask for it and then wait to 'see the manager' or someone who can deal with the request. Such an interview is seen by most consumers as a forbidding experience and most would therefore prefer to avoid it. Even in the withdrawal of their own funds, today many people would rather queue at an ATM than use the human teller (especially if they have only limited balances and do not want the embarrassment of making only a small withdrawal). Moreover, the new model ATMs in Japan and the USA have actually been programmed to provide customer assistance, a friendly voice and a picture of a girl who looks pretty and knows how to smile. As a vehicle for the marketing of a wide range of services the traditional branch is little short of being a disaster with usually only poorly positioned, inadequate point of sale literature available to the consumer to tell him or her what services the bank does provide.

With the development of so many alternative customer driven

delivery points, banks will have to face the major task of making their branches sufficiently attractive for consumers to want to visit them. In the retail trade, for example, one store group, when moving premises, has a deliberate policy of selling or leasing its old sites to banks or building societies in the expectation that this will reduce consumer traffic flow in the area.

There are many experiments at present taking place within the industry to improve the image of the bank branch, to make it less intimidating and easier for the customer to purchase the bank's range of services. As a result there will be the development of many open plan service branches, with specialist officers in the substantially increased customer area of the bank, while the area given over to the back office will be shrunk. However, traffic-generating products or services will also be needed and these are likely to include insurance broking, possibly equity dealing, real estate brokerage and travel services.

Consumers actually only require a limited number of such full service branches. They want convenience for basic transactions, notably cash deposits and withdrawals. Hence these services are likely to be provided more by machines and by limited service branches. Other services, such as insurance quotations, loan applications and the like, will be provided by terminal-driven systems which can either be customer activated or used by relatively unskilled employees.

Retail store based branches are also likely to become common with normal retail opening hours rather than conventional bank hours. The danger for the banks will be that the retailers themselves may decide to operate such branches as Sears Roebuck and Ford Motor Company do via their First Nationwide Subsidiary in conjunction with K-Mart in the USA. In the UK, clearly retailers such as Marks and Spencer, Burton Group, Storehouse and possibly some of the major superstore operators, will enter the market for at least some retail financial services. As a result, bankers, too, will increasingly need to look upon their branch networks as retail store sites rather than listed buildings, and consider measures such as sales and profitability per square foot as management tools. In the retail industry those stores that cannot operate profitably get closed down. Applying the same criteria to retail business bank branches, some substantial rationalisation of the existing branch networks of the main clearing banks can be predicted over the next several years.

Summary

Retail banking has been something of a Cinderella activity within the industry in recent years. Rather, the emphasis has been on developing corporate banking business. Today, the major banks are increasingly specialising and creating corporate banking units, not merely to cover the large corporate market, but also to provide dedicated services to the very important middle market. Corporate accounts are therefore being withdrawn from the conventional branch networks and placed with specialist corporate branches.

As a result, the traditional branch network is being forced to focus on providing a range of services to the retail market. The relative success of Citibank's Individual Bank has also stimulated renewed interest amongst bankers in the profit opportunities that may exist within this market. To be successful, however, the industry must carefully examine its position with consumers and understand what the needs of key segments are and how these might be met. To endeavour to continue to provide all services to all men through the traditional branch delivery system is a recipe which invites failure.

Rather, it will become increasingly important to segment the retail market and decide which sectors one wishes to focus on; then to design an appropriate mix of products and services that each chosen segment wishes to purchase through an appropriate delivery system, which may or may not be built around the traditional branch. Moreover it should be recognised that consumers will not, *ad infinitum*, allow the banks to operate with a high cost structure, supported by a system of bundled service pricing, offering inconvenient operating hours and indifferent consideration of customer needs. This is especially true when new entrant competitors may offer better facilities, innovative services, a pleasant environment, and superior convenience. In order to be successful, the bank of tomorrow will need to grow much more like some of the retailers who may emerge as important competitors making the purchasing of financial services a pleasant experience rather than a necessary chore.

Robert W. Carlton-Porter, ACIB

Bob Carlton-Porter joined English China Clays Plc in September 1983 and was appointed Finance Director in 1984. He joined ECC from Hoechst UK where his role was mainly finance but with commercial involvements. His early career lay mostly in banking where he worked in line management both in the UK and overseas.

He is a Member of the Institute of Marketing, a Fellow of the British Institute of Management, an Associate of the Chartered Institute of Bankers and a Founder Fellow of the Association of Corporate Treasurers. Until recently he was Chairman of the Editorial Committee of *The Treasurer*, the official journal of the Association of Corporate Treasurers, and he is now Vice-Chairman of the ACT Council.

Robert Carlton-Porter

2. THE CORPORATE CUSTOMER'S VIEW

Contents

"If only we'd borrowed as much as Brazil!"

THE CORPORATE CUSTOMER'S VIEW

Growing professionalism

As a practitioner of the ever changing art of financial management, I want to talk about corporate finance in practice, but first let me set the scene between ourselves as corporates and you as lenders.

In a world where one week has become a very long time it is necessary for the practitioner to be more specific in identifying his corporate requirements and for the provider of finance to become a great deal more aware of the peculiar circumstances of that customer. I am mindful that any critique that is done with the benefit of hindsight may leave an impression of perfection – of inspired analysis followed by purposeful execution. In reality it is usually far less so – we all have had our share of failures, false starts and fumblings, and it all seems to take far longer than it should. With professionalism now becoming the norm on both sides of the lending barrier our hopes must be that in future we can learn from these lessons and provide a firm financial basis of choice from which to expand our industries worldwide.

The corporate finance function

Corporate customers vary in their financial needs. An obvious statement but one that is frequently overlooked when the generalisations of advertising – promising all – prevail. The bespoke approach is the expectation of industrial companies, whether they be multi-nationals, European based, or indigenous in nature, and irrespective of whether they are large, medium or small in their needs.

So what are the key elements involved in corporate finance? They include, in no particular order, the Stock Market and equity issues of all types, public debt issues, debt capacity, cost of capital and dividend policy, mergers and acquisitions, joint ventures and divestments and defence against predatory takeover, investment appraisal, forecasting and budgeting, pension funding and investment, risk management and insurance, tax, and the implications of other related financial information for the organisation of the finance function. As an aside, there is a growing trend for more and more treasurers to be promoted to finance director, quite a few without an accountancy qualification. There is obviously, therefore, a growing consensus that treasury management is compulsory experience for the successful finance director. The finance director's job is all about decision making, as is treasury management, whereas, for the most part, the pure accounting function in industry (as opposed to the performance-orientated controllership function) is about recording in a satisfactory fashion the events of the past. This is not meant to be in any way disparaging but is intended to emphasise to you all that your customer is changing rapidly, and, for your part, developing the right approach and service needs a good deal of thought.

The changing environment

At this stage it is relevant to make some mention of the major reform of the City of London and its several markets. One of the principal objectives has been the desire to ensure London's future role as a pre-eminent international financial centre. The enhancement of London's competitive advantage is seen as an important consequence of the far-reaching changes in the Stock Exchange and in the regulatory apparatus established by the Financial Services Act. Over the last 25 years or so, the rise of Eurocurrency business to be today the City's main international activity, hinges not just on expertise but also on its time-zone position, coupled with a traditional concentration of ancillary services in law, accounting, shipping, commodity markets and financial printing. The corporate customer has long recognised the importance of the financial services provided by the City and now that the constraints imposed by exchange controls are lifted, the domestic fiscal framework largely clarified, and post 'Big Bang' globalisation a fact, future success depends on a greater understanding of the partnership which can be forged between the City and Industry. Financial services as an economic activity cannot succeed in isolation and the City's competitive edge can be eroded by a stronger national commitment from Tokyo and New York.

Adapting to change

The revolution in communications technology has changed the face of traditional banking and investment activity. Savers, investors, borrowers and lenders around the world now enjoy instant access to financial information, prices and market alternatives, due largely to the speed at which electronic transmission makes such data available. Under these circumstances, traditional markets can no longer provide the liquidity demanded by a rapidly expanding clientele. The development of sophisticated financial techniques has removed many of the natural barriers to the free movement of capital and neutralised the impact of foreign exchange exposure in cross-border investment activity. To meet these challenges, London has to adapt its institutions without destroying their traditional strength.

Up to now I have concentrated on the current the scene – remembering that the strength of the participants and the market's products themselves are forever changing. So let me turn to how I see corporate requirements and therefore bank products evolving.

Perhaps a few words on domestic, as distinct from institutional, international banking. The UK has a highly sophisticated interconnected network of branches, perhaps unique in the Western world in its characteristics, and the lengthy two-day clearing on cheques is fast becoming an anachronism. We hope that the development by the Bankers Automated Clearing System of something which can virtually replace cheques will be in sight as soon as the totally impractical reference field of some 24 characters is extended to, say, 100 characters. The above are outstanding examples where progress has not been attained – the corporates cannot understand why. They may seem minor items but they represent major cost or cost saving areas, and it is galling to see major expenditure on credit card access while systems affecting all corporates are neglected. The growing specialisation of corporate lending into Head Office or Regional Office functions is welcomed, but this will become obsolete itself unless specialisation can be extended from pure banking to reflect the wider financial services of the newly acquired Stock Market firms.

These criticisms aside the clearing system is sound and reliable and suffers only from the fact that banks seem remarkably coy when developing services aimed at the corporate. Collaboration with the user would ensure they offer the right services at the right time. The user has choice – as indeed do all our customers. This leads to pricing of services in the domestic network. Some 10 years ago I made a comment that the time would shortly come when loadings on corporate sterling lending were at a level where they represented just a turnaround fee and that the marketing and proper costing of services would become the norm. That is, and will be, the trend today; not that the provision of finance is incidental but its provision is in relative balance to the overall purposes communicated between lender and borrower.

Over the broad markets, therefore, the provision of the right services is common to all forms of corporate needs and it would be pointless for me to go through all the ramifications of Foreign Exchange, NIFS, RUFS, ECUs, commercial paper, medium term notes, zero coupon bonds *et al* as I am sure that you are aware of all these in varying degrees of depth. It is not important that you offer all these as a bank but it is important that you are a major player in a particular field. For example, the number of banks offering sterling commercial paper is, I believe, around 20 – the number actually rated as major players is 3–5. Any corporate would want to be with the keenest player. Likewise a Euro-CP programme without a Swiss bank involved is like Hamlet without the Prince.

So what 'sells' the bank is what keeps us all in a job: 'proven performance in the market'. Therefore I return again to my theme of choice. One of the most disagreeable aspects of the current mergers is the implication that many of these collectivisations of existing services are being promoted on the basis of a divine right to the business principle, rather than to be there to help and provide a service. No thinking corporate will ever be attracted to 'one-stop' financial services, although 'choice' may attract a greater concentration of services under one financial services umbrella than heretofore. But business gained should not be taken for granted. Let me not give an impression that relationships do not matter – they do – and my experience is that good relationships run hand in hand with cost effective and competitive services. After all, isn't trust the basis of a relationship and trust inspires both parties to say 'no can do' when appropriate as well as 'can do'?

Turning to the ever-challenging question of pricing: is this critical? When all is said and done the bottom line is the judgemental criterion for all engaged in the business of commerce, so pricing is a critical aspect. But pricing has to be viewed in the context of the objective as a whole and the more worldwide the operations of the corporate client the more knowledgeable he will be of local costings and their disparity with those acceptable in the UK. My own company has been through the rigours of a Rights Issue, USA Commercial Paper and Euro Commercial Paper, Ratings and US Listing in the past couple of years and has learnt from those experiences that a policy of demanding an up front budget on cost is the right and proper way to control matters. One worrying aspect of these experiences has been that legal bodies do tend to dominate the costs which arise and perhaps there is a message to you that a firm knowledge of what you want from your lawyers can mitigate expenses. A legal adviser with a seemingly free hand can make conclusion of a deal which is mutually agreeable to you and your corporate client a tortuous experience.

Having mentioned aspirations in the USA, I suppose a brief mention of the effects of deregulation and disintermediation would not be amiss. Neither aspects should hold out any fears for corporates; in fact on balance they offer many advantages. There should be no illusions that deregulation brings a lack of regulations; in fact, experience has shown that as corporates pursue new concepts of finance, legal and fiscal requirements fill the corporate's file.

Earlier I alluded to the collectivisation of corporate financial services in fewer hands and thinking corporates' aversion to this. Much stress has been placed on the financial muscle of the major institutions and therefore on the need to see big as beautiful. The message of resilience has been somewhat dampened however by some extremely rapid withdrawals from UK gilts market-making; resilience has its limits and risk aversion still prevails. Muscle does not necessarily always go hand in hand with creativity – indeed it could be said that the contrary is usually the case. I, for one, see markets continuing to be liquid; and therefore smaller, more creative and personal houses will continue to have adequate 'friends' to provide the finances to complete well structured deals. Despite all the fanfare surrounding 'Big Bang', financing remains a personal contact relationship matter. Corporates do not seek vastly peopled treasury functions as treasury is involved in many of the confidential aspirations of companies – therefore the fewer, but more capable, hands the better. There is sometimes a tendency for bankers to arrive in numbers in answer to a specific query. Numbers rarely beget confidentiality and it is better that the bank's relationship manager seeks to grasp the roots of the request and structures his answering team accordingly. This is a fundamental weakness of regional corporate offices and the reason why time and again corporates go direct to an inner expert they know.

It is a rare occurrence for corporates to abandon relationship banks, and change at operational levels in any event will be costly. In the field of advice, however, the business will go to the imaginative and reliable source and therefore change will be inevitable unless the bank is unusually adroit, responsive and fast on its feet.

A good relationship can enable the bank to obtain indications of future needs and the way ahead. If the bank's services are developing along parallel lines, all to the good. If the bank can advise on future developments envisaged in, for example, electronics or currency availability these can be considered as part of the planning exercise. We all have to seek an end to working in total isolation; the confidentiality of discussions between bankers and clients will be preserved by the interests of both; working together produces better results for everyone. We all seek the same thing – the continuity which leads to a prosperous future.

Mark Boleat

Mark Boleat joined the Building Societies Association as Assistant Secretary (Public Relations) in January 1974 and subsequently held a number of positions before being appointed Secretary-General in September 1986. He was appointed to the new position of Director-General in June 1987.

He is Secretary-General of the International Union of Building Societies and Savings Associations and Managing Director of the European Federation of Building Societies. He has been a consultant on housing finance for the United Nations and the OECD and has given many papers on housing finance at international conferences. He is editor of *Housing Finance International* and an author of numerous publications and articles on housing finance.

Outside the BSA, he is involved in the voluntary housing movement, serving as Chairman of Tennant Housing Trust and Vice-Chairman of Circle 33 Housing Trust.

Mark Boleat

3. THE COMPETITOR'S VIEW

Contents

[31]

"We'd like to reach a similar agreement with
Marks and Spencer"

THE COMPETITOR'S VIEW

Introduction

The largest British clearing banks are all international financial conglomerates, and most other British banks also operate in a number of financial markets. Some of these markets have comparatively little in common with others. For example, the only common link between the British retail savings market and the financing of international trade is money itself, and the characteristics needed for the two types of business are very different.

British building societies, by contrast, operate in fairly narrowly defined retail financial markets in Britain. In these markets their main competitors are the clearing banks and the competition between the two sets of institutions is an interesting case study of the relative position of general financial institutions and those confined to more specific services.

This paper concentrates predominantly on British building societies, illustrating how they have been successful over the years, discussing the reasons for this success and considering in detail the present market position of banks as against building societies in particular, and other financial institutions generally. Finally, it speculates on future developments.

The success of the building societies

A brief examination of the statistics is enough to show how successful British building societies have been in the post-war period. In the markets in which they have operated they have inexorably increased market share, they have established an excellent reputation with the public, and, as institutions, they have grown both steadily and profitably without the traumas that many other financial institutions have suffered. In the savings market it is estimated that building societies accounted for only 10 per cent of personal sector liquid deposits in 1950, with the banks and national savings holding the other 90 per cent almost equally. Building societies have steadily increased their market share such that they now hold about 50 per cent of the liquid assets of the personal sector. This increase in market share was initially at the expense of national savings but more recently has also been at the expense of the banks.

This performance is perhaps put in better perspective when it is realised that building societies do not, for the most part, compete for transaction accounts, banks still having a near monopoly here. If the market for liquid savings is considered then societies probably have a market share of around two-thirds. This dominance of the retail savings market by a group of specialised housing finance institutions is unique in the industrialised world.

The societies' record in the mortgage market has been every bit as spectacular. Detailed figures are not available for the share of the mortgage market as they are for the share of the savings market. However, an examination of building society lending on new housing, when compared with the number of new houses completed, shows that societies steadily increased their share of total mortgage business from perhaps 60 per cent in the 1950s to 80 per cent by the early 1980s. The latest figures show that societies have some three quarters of outstanding mortgage loans.

Societies have been extremely successful in two markets which themselves have been growing rapidly, and therefore they have increased rapidly in size, employing more and more people and earning an ever greater volume of profits. They have emerged from being fairly insignificant peripheral institutions immediately after the war to major players in the British financial markets today.

In addition to this, societies have managed to remain popular institutions enjoying a far better public image than the banks. Societies are perceived as being more friendly to deal with and they do not have the remoteness that many people feel about their banks. This has been illustrated by a number of market research surveys.

Reasons for success

There are a number of reasons why building societies have been very successful institutions, particularly in relation to the banks.

Those in the building society industry would naturally like to feel that their success is because they have been incredibly efficient and that the banks have not been able to match them. While there may be some truth in this, there are more fundamental factors and, simply put, it can be said that building societies have enjoyed exceptionally favourable market conditions which they have exploited with supreme efficiency.

Societies have been fortunate in that the law has, until recently, confined them to operating in two markets, but those two markets have been, for various reasons, rapidly growing. The societies' ultimate product is, of course, the mortgage loan and few markets in Britain have been more favoured than the mortgage market. It has been favoured not just by one factor but by a combination.

First, most people take out mortgage loans in order to purchase houses and the house purchase market has been particularly buoyant. In Britain there is no market rented sector of housing and accordingly there is an artificial demand for owner-occupation. The proportion of homes which are owner-occupied has increased from 29 per cent in 1950 to well over 60 per cent now and seems likely to increase to about 75 per cent by the turn of the century. In Britain people become owner-occupiers at a very early age and no other industrialised country can show the same proportion of owner-occupation among 25 year olds as Britain. Of all countries in the industrialised world, Britain has also shown the most rapid growth in owner-occupation.

The growth in demand for home ownership was accentuated, during the 1970s in particular, by the favourable tax treatment of owner-occupied homes. For a time during that decade the only investment that people could make which was certain to keep pace with inflation, and which was not subject to Capital Gains Tax was their own home. Housing therefore became an investment good as well as a consumption good.

This artificial demand for home-ownership has naturally stimulated an artificial demand for mortgage loans, the main product of building societies. However, mortgage loans themselves have also been favourably treated for tax purposes. Mortgage interest is tax deductible and until 1974 that tax deductibility was unlimited. Until the last few years, most people could, effectively, obtain full tax relief on the loan which they took out to purchase their home.

Mortgage lending has also been exceptionally safe for financial institutions, partly because the lack of a market rented sector has virtually removed the risk of a large scale collapse of the owner-occupied housing market in Britain, such as that which has occurred, for example, in Belgium and the Netherlands. The availability of supplementary benefit to meet the mortgage interest payments of unemployed home owners has similarly helped to underpin the housing finance market. The combination of these factors has meant that mortgage losses have been minimal and therefore interest rates have been kept at a low level thus further stimulating demand.

Indeed, the favourable tax treatment of mortgage loans together with the safe nature of mortgage lending has meant that most people have been able to borrow on mortgage at a lower interest rate than they have been able to obtain on their savings. This has been particularly true for higher rate tax payers who have been able to enjoy a combination of tax free investment in Government instruments and tax relieved debt.

The mortgage market has therefore boomed, growing by some 18 per cent a year, yet it has remained an exceptionally safe market, losses being miniscule compared with those recorded on other forms of lending.

Given such a favourable market situation, one would expect large numbers of lenders seeking to compete in this market. Here, building societies enjoyed their greatest advantage. The fact is that for much of the 1960s and 1970s their natural competitors were prevented from competing. In most housing finance markets in the world one finds a variety of lenders including commercial banks, cooperative banks, savings banks, specialist mortgage banks, and sometimes building society type institutions. In Britain there has been no cooperative bank sector, presumably because industrialisation in Britain occurred earlier than in most other countries. The savings banks hardly existed in terms of lending until recently and generally the fact that they were under government control prevented them from competing effectively with building societies. The commercial banks were subject to a variety of constraints operated as part of monetary policy throughout the 1960s and 1970s, all of which discouraged them from seeking to increase their deposits or expand their lending. The banks reacted, not surprisingly, by withdrawing to some extent from the personal market, this being exemplified by their decisions to close on Saturday mornings and also by their paying derisory rates of interest on savings accounts.

The reasons for the success of building societies are therefore apparent. Societies operated by law in two tightly confined markets yet due to a variety of unrelated factors these markets were rapidly growing and their natural competitors in these markets were prevented from competing with them. This idyllic state of affairs led to the rapid growth of the building society industry and by the early 1980s it had taken its place as one of the key financial sectors in the British economy.

The changing competitive environment

The situation has changed dramatically over the past few years. Building societies are now being challenged in markets which they made their own and in turn the societies have moved into other markets. The reasons for the break down of the barriers between financial markets and institutions have been well described elsewhere and will be only briefly summarised here. Technology has made barriers between markets difficult to sustain and has also made non-market policy instruments ineffective. The corset was rendered ineffective by banks simply guaranteeing loans made from one of their customers to another rather than making the loans and accepting deposits themselves. More sophisticated computer systems enabled such constraints to be overcome more effectively.

Governments also realised that artificial constraints inhibited the efficient functioning of financial institutions. Banks had responded quite sensibly, from their point of view, to the constraints imposed on them by reducing the level of customer service. What was the point of opening on Saturday mornings and offering good interest rates to depositors if the main effect of this was to be penalised by the Government? The break-up of the bank cartel in the 1970s was perceived to have increased the efficiency of the banking industry and the newly elected Conservative Government in 1979 was anxious to build on this experience.

The abolition of exchange controls in 1979 led inevitably to the abolition of the corset in 1980 and for the first time the banks were free to compete with building societies for savings and mortgage loans without being subject to any artificial balance sheet constraints. The steady decline in the banks' share of personal business was beginning to cause problems. The banks had become increasingly reliant on wholesale rather than retail deposits and, more generally, there was no point in having some 12,000 branches if one was not predominantly in the retail market. The banks were therefore anxious to regain their place in the personal market and perceived that this could be done relatively easily because they already had the customers, the staff and the branches and all that they needed were the products. Accordingly, the banks attacked the mortgage market vigorously and also offered more attractive savings accounts. Inevitably, as with any new entrant into the market, the banks did not make a complete success of it and indeed their early experience in the mortgage market was somewhat messy, with surges of lending being followed by equally rapid withdrawals from the market. However, it is now clear that banks are in the mortgage market to stay, they have developed many of the innovations in the market and, moreover, they have forced building societies to reconsider their pricing policies.

The banks are not the only new entrants in the mortgage market. The advent of a more competitive mortgage market has encouraged a number of institutional investors to set up specialist mortgage lending companies, funded on the wholesale markets, which obtain mortgage business through intermediaries.

There is, therefore, a very competitive mortgage market with building societies being but one of a number of types of supplier. There is virtually no brand loyalty towards particular mortgage lenders and indeed a mortgage loan is a product that is difficult to differentiate. One mortgage is much the same as another just as one potato is much the same as another.

As building societies have experienced strong competition in their traditional markets, so they have been able to move into new markets themselves. Any institution coming under threat in one market has to look at whether it has comparative advantage in other markets. Building societies built on their strengths, their strong customer base, popular public image, large scale branch networks, and dominance of the retail savings and mortgage markets. New technology meant that it became easier for societies to offer limited money transmission facilities, often in conjunction with smaller banks or other financial institutions. Societies were able to use the latest technology to install more efficient automated teller machines than the banks. In the mortgage market, societies exploited the opportunities to capture related business such as insurance broking and arranging unsecured loans.

There has been a rebundling of services in the savings and mortgage markets. A competitive mortgage market has shifted the balance of power away from the providers of mortgage funds towards the providers of mortgage applicants and the estate agency business is accordingly undergoing a rapid change with agents themselves moving into the financial services market and financial institutions building up networks of estate agencies both to secure their source of mortgage business and in addition, related business, insurance for example. The savings market and the market for money transmission services are becoming merged with the customer now expecting an account which offers both a high rate of interest and money transmission services.

In this new market place building societies are less well placed than they were to provide mortgages, but very well placed to provide other financial services.

However, societies were constrained from competing fully by a legal framework which dated back to 1874 and which, broadly speaking, prevented them from doing anything other than making mortgage loans, attracting retail deposits and providing services directly incidental to those main functions. This problem for societies was rectified by the passage through Parliament of legislation which became the Building Societies Act 1986 which freed societies to make unsecured loans and to provide the full range of house-buying and financial services.

By early 1987 both banks and building societies had been freed from the constraints which prevented them from competing across the full range of retail business and market conditions had changed dramatically over the few previous years. It is against this backdrop that one can examine the present market position of banks *vis à vis* building societies in particular.

The present market position of banks

Building societies certainly see banks as being their major competitors although they are certainly not their only competitors. In the mortgage market the running is sometimes being made by the new mortgage companies which have found a perfect niche in the market and which are sensibly operating by obtaining their funds at the lowest cost, taking the most profitable mortgage business, and keeping their operating costs to a minimum.

In competing with building societies, banks have three main advantages. The first is their huge customer base. They have more customers than building societies, this in turn reflecting their total domination of the money transmission business. Only in the past few years have societies begun to offer current accounts and, even so, most people who have such accounts with building societies also have them with banks. Armed with the huge number of people with bank accounts and with what is still a very large share of the personal sector money transmission business, banks have the essential ingredients to offer a wide range of financial services: that is, the customer base and control of the key financial product, the current account.

The banks also have comprehensive branch networks, the largest in the world for big commercial banks. They have offices in all of the large cities and towns and their branch networks spread to suburban areas and small towns (although obviously the same services cannot be offered through small branches as through larger ones).

The banks have begun to use these advantages by cross-selling products. Direct mail is rapidly becoming a major method of marketing financial services. It is cheap and is most likely to attract sophisticated customers who can often be most profitable. By contrast, selling a product through branches is very expensive and people who actually have the time to visit branches to discuss financial products may well be those who are not likely to be very profitable to a financial institution.

Notwithstanding those great advantages, the banks also have a number of disadvantages. The first of these is that although they have a large customer base, one suspects that they do not have the computer systems to enable them readily to use customer information for marketing purposes. This is clearly illustrated by the fact that banks seem to spend much time selling, through direct mail, services which people already have. The TSB and, to take a non-bank example, American Express, must spend vast amounts of money marketing Visa cards and American Express cards to people who already have them. Clearly they do not have a marketing system which enables them to cut out existing customers. But it is not sufficient just to know who is one's customer. Rather, one needs to know a fair bit about the customer in terms of income, other financial products purchased, and so on. One understands that banks, like building societies, are endeavouring to deal with this situation by completely reorganising the form in which information is held: basically switching it from account based information to customer based information. Until the banks successfully do this, they are not able to make effective use of their customer base.

A second constraint on the banks is that because they have been first in the market for a number of services, in particular, automated teller machines, they now have the oldest technology; whereas new institutions in the market, like building societies, can take advantage of the latest technology. Building societies can now provide money transmission services every bit as good and probably better than most of those offered by banks. They are able to do so either on their own account or by using banks to clear cheques and here one should note that the status of a clearing bank is not of the slightest interest to the retail customer. It may be of interest in the banking world as to whether a building society is a member of the clearing system but all the customer is concerned about is whether he has a cheque which will be accepted. The fact that it has to go through two stages before being cleared rather than one is probably an advantage rather than a disadvantage if it takes longer to clear cheques.

A final disadvantage that the banks have, one shared by building societies, although not to the same extent, is that branches are an increasingly inefficient method of delivering retail financial services. Broadly speaking, it can be said that it must be inefficient to use a physical location to sell a non-physical product such as a loan, a savings account or money transmission services. Branches were certainly essential when there were no ATMs because they were a method of paying in cash to a bank and getting cash out. Now, however, people can service all of their cash requirements through ATMs. Of course, it is true that some people prefer to use a branch but providing cash services through a branch is very much more expensive than providing them through an ATM because staff have to be employed who for some of their time will not be fully utilized. This clearly cannot be profitable for the bank.

Some customers, of course, want to discuss products that they are buying and this can be particularly inefficient for the institution. Any bank manager should be charging out his time at at least £50 an hour and a half-hour chat with an elderly customer would have to generate a huge amount of business in order to pay for his time.

There is a grave danger that bank branches will suffer in much the same way as some high street shopping centres, and indeed trends in the two are related. Increasingly, out of town shopping centres are becoming more important and large supermarkets with car parking facilities are pushing traditional high streets out of business. Of course, the high streets are still necessary for people who live locally and do not have cars. However, a characteristic shared by many people who do not have cars is that they do not have much money either and one finds some high streets increasingly being pushed down-market in terms of the shops that are there and the people that are using them. The downward spiral feeds on itself. Meanwhile, the more affluent customers are travelling fairly short distances by car to do all their shopping in a convenient manner.

Most sophisticated customers, who can be profitable bank or building society customers, never set foot in their branches. Conversely the people who do use branches, in many cases, are not profitable: for example, a small trader bringing in masses of coins which he wants paid into his account or taking out masses of change, and the person who has got nothing better to do than to spend half an hour talking to branch staff about investing a few hundred pounds in one product or another.

Banks and building societies have both probably got more branches than they need to sell the services which they are now offering, but for banks the problem is greater because they have much more investment tied up in these branches than the building societies.

Building societies therefore see banks as their main competitors because they have the customers, the branches, and the expertise. But, each of these advantages is now slightly tempered and building societies can compete effectively against banks in all of the retail markets. Societies do not have as many branches but then, clearly, they no longer need them. They do not have the same expertise, but that expertise can be relatively easily acquired by linking with other financial institutions to provide, for example, cheque book accounts, and by the use of the latest technology which enables societies to provide comprehensive insurance broking services through their branches without employing any expert staff in those branches at all.

Societies feel that when they are selling products through branches they have the great advantage of a much better public image and this spills over into any products which they sell. Building societies are fortunate because they sell popular products whereas banks sell unpopular products. While there is every justification for making bank charges the sad fact is that the public does not understand this (although it has to be said that this is partly because the banks, or at least some of them, have done their best to ensure that the public does not understand it by continually referring to free banking).

The balance of competitive advantage between banks and building societies is a very fine one. The banks have found the mortgage market to be a profitable one and are also now much more of a threat in the retail savings market. They have the customer base, the branch network, the staff and the expertise to be major players in the retail financial services market. However, they have more restructuring to do in order to take advantage of this market place. That restructuring has to include branch closures and radical changes in their method of operation. Building societies, by contrast, are still on the way up. They have just been empowered to offer many new services and they are expanding rather than contracting. As new entrants they start with significant advantages, including their huge customer base which they are better able to utilise for marketing purposes than the banks, and they are not so encumbered by employing people and facilities no longer appropriate to the market place.

The future

How will the banks fare against their competitors in this brave new world? In the retail financial markets, they will certainly find building societies their strongest although not their only competitors. Modern technology and the removal of regulatory constraints mean that it is open to almost any institution to provide retail financial services including current accounts, mortgages, savings accounts, life insurance products and so on. The retailers are particularly well placed here and there is also room for niche institutions concentrating on particular highly specialised lines of business and obtaining their business through links with other organisations.

The banks can be expected to gain market share in those areas where they are currently not very strong. One would expect them to be able easily to maintain a 20 per cent share of mortgage business and, moreover, for this to be very profitable for them. At a push, they could possibly increase their market share to 30 per cent although this might entail some securitisation of mortgage loans given the heavy capital backing which the banks are required to maintain for their mortgage lending business – a far higher capital backing than that required of building societies.

When they obtain mortgage business, banks can be expected to sell ancillary products such as unsecured loans and life and buildings insurance. These are all areas where the banks can be expected to gain business over the next few years.

Conversely, banks can be expected to lose business in areas where building societies now enjoy a strong comparative advantage. In the same way that banks were artificially prevented from competing with building societies in the savings and mortgage markets in the 1960s and 1970s, so building societies were artificially prevented from competing with banks in the markets for money transmission services, unsecured loans and credit cards. In advanced industrialised countries, building societies are almost alone in being significant savings institutions without the full range of retail financial services. Until the new Act, societies were prevented from offering credit cards, unsecured loans and reasonable money transmission facilities. Now, societies have been freed to offer all of these products.

Unsecured loans are one area where building societies can be expected to do very well. In the past, societies found themselves in the absurd position of giving people mortgage loans to buy their houses but when those people asked to borrow a little extra to purchase furniture and fittings the societies directed them across the road to the bank to be charged a much higher rate of interest. Building societies can now be expected to capture this business.

Similarly, building societies can be expected to become major players in the credit card market. They can use their strong customer base, which they are much better equipped to exploit than are the banks, to provide Visa or some other form of credit card; already societies are beginning to make moves in this direction.

Perhaps the banks have most to fear in respect of their core retail business, the cheque book account. The banks have not had to work very hard to get current account business in the past because they have enjoyed a monopoly. It has been almost impossible for many people to be paid or for student grants to be used without a bank account. Now, building societies are able to offer similar accounts and, because they can design these products *de novo* they can often make them more attractive to the customer and more profitable for themselves. For building societies it is not a question of imposing charges on those who previously had not been charged because societies have previously not had current account customers. They can gear their pricing structure to what they consider appropriate and capture the type of business they want rather than be left with the type of business that nobody actually wants.

Societies have been remarkably successful in the market for childrens' savings, now having some 40 per cent of all children as their investors. Societies are not doing this out of any charitable motive of teaching children about money management, although that does come into it. Rather, when those children reach the age when they want full banking services, building societies will already have them as customers and will seek to capture them as banking customers before the banks get a look in. The banks are well aware of this and it is for this reason that they too have entered the children's market.

Building societies have a natural place in the market for money transmission services just as banks have a natural place in the mortgage market. Building societies can be expected to compete aggressively for retail banking business and will take a significant proportion of it away from banks, while they in turn lose share of the mortgage market to the banks.

This is the market situation one would have expected. Comparative advantage has changed because of technological developments and deregulation, and each institution now has to discover the markets in which it is best placed and how it can best exploit those markets. This might mean turning away from markets that have been successful in the past because new market conditions might not allow the same institutions to be as successful in those markets as before.

The building societies gained when the banks were heavily regulated in the 1960s and 1970s. In the early 1980s the banks were deregulated but the building societies were shackled by an outmoded legal framework. Now the building societies have also been freed from their constraints and for the first time banks and building societies are completely free to compete across the whole range of retail financial services, relatively unencumbered by regulatory distortions. There is no particular reason to expect banks or building societies to come out on top as a group. Rather, one would expect the most efficient banks and building societies to do the best and the least efficient institutions to do very badly indeed.

Were it not for the special legal status of building societies, one would expect a merger between banks and building societies. However, given the constitution of building societies under the 1986 Act this would be very difficult to effect. A building society can convert to a public company but it could do so, and lose its own independence, only by persuading 50 per cent of its investing shareholders to vote in favour. This would be extremely difficult, although perhaps not impossible. However, one should not rule out one or two medium-sized building societies going for the conversion option, perhaps linking with other financial institutions which wish to expand their retail financial business.

The banks will continue to be the dominant institutions in the British financial markets. However, in the retail markets, with the exception of money transmission services, they lost that dominance a long time ago. I doubt if they will regain it. The retail financial markets will form a significant but not huge part of their business. They will have to face very strong competition from building societies which will be specialists in this market and are perceived as being so. Banks will have to work very hard in order to maintain, let alone improve, their performance in the retail financial markets. Building societies have no other markets to turn to given their present legal position whereas banks, if they do not like the British retail market, have other markets in which they can use their funds and their staff. Perhaps this factor might prove to be the crucial one in the long term.

Brian Pitman, FCIB

Brian Pitman took up his present position as Chief Executive of Lloyds Bank in December 1983.

He has spent most of his career with Lloyds Bank, with a wide range of experience in domestic and international banking, including spells in Europe and the USA. He was appointed Assistant General Manager, Corporate Services Division, in 1973, and a Joint General Manager, responsible for the bank's London banking business, in 1975.

In 1976 he was appointed an Executive Director of Lloyds Bank International, responsible for the UK and Asia-Pacific Divisions, and in 1978 he became Deputy Chief Executive of the Lloyds Bank Group.

He is a Director of Lloyds Bank Plc, the National Bank of New Zealand and Lloyds Merchant Bank Holdings Limited. He is a Fellow of the Chartered Institute of Bankers.

Brian Pitman

4. A BANKER'S VIEW

Contents

*"I introduced a building society executive
to a bank manager"*

A BANKER'S VIEW

Introduction

After years sheltered from the full rigour of market competition, the challenge now confronting banks is how to survive and prosper in an evolving free market for financial services.

Competition, deregulation and technology are changing the shape of the financial services business. Markets are open. Barriers to entry are coming down. New competitors are arriving from all directions. Excess capacity is emerging in an already crowded market place and severe price competition is developing.

The risks to participants in the new market environment have risen considerably. Yet profit margins have declined. The relatively low price earnings multiples for bank shares in Britain and the USA reflect investors' doubts.

A new definition of success is beginning to take hold among bankers. For decades the chart bankers first turned to was the one listing size of assets. The top bank was the one with the largest assets and it was not unusual for a bank to go to considerable lengths in order to remain at the top of its group. All this is coming to an end. The new definition of success is market value and it is resulting in some dramatic shifts in perception as to who is winning. Measured by market value at the end of 1986, no British bank ranked among the top twenty-five in the world. One West German bank and one Swiss bank were each twice as big as the largest British bank and one Japanese bank was more than five times as big.

Market value is becoming so important because many observers see the possibility of a wave of bank mergers and acquisitions. Those banks which have strong share prices and high market value will be absorbing banks which do not. But the task of increasing the market value of bank shares is much more difficult than the old aim of increasing the size of a bank's assets. Only those banks that produce a return on equity in excess of their cost of equity will create shareholder value. Here the British banks have been at a disadvantage because the relatively high rate of inflation in the UK has pushed up the cost of equity. If the British economy continues to improve and inflation comes down, the market value of British banks could receive a boost.

Ultimately, the challenge is about survival. In a rapidly changing environment, the gap between the best and the worst performers is likely to widen: the weakest will go to the wall. It is a time of high risk, but also a time of exceptional opportunity. Those banks which get it right will emerge stronger than ever.

I would like to discuss what I see as the key success factors under five headings: the strategic challenge, the profitability challenge, the capital challenge, the technology challenge and, above all, the people challenge.

The strategic challenge

A bank's strategy has to start with its customers. You can only build value for your shareholders if you can create value for your customers. In today's competitive free-for-all, customers will shop around until they find the best possible service at the finest price. Superior returns and leadership can only be earned by delivering superior value to customers.

Marketing philosophy is continually evolving. A few years ago, the approach was one of mass marketing: today it is about market segmentation and market positioning. In the past, banks were advised to carry a full product line; today, we are tending to prune product lines and are harder-nosed about which products make money. There is more interest in a profitable product line than a full product line. Looking back, marketing meant building sales volume for every product. In the 1980s we know that some of our businesses are not growth businesses and should not be run for growth. They should be run for maintenance, or for harvesting. Ten years ago, we said pricing should be based on cost, now we are saying pricing should be based more on perceived value. In the 1970s we thought banks should be in many markets and not necessarily dominate any. Today, banks are advised to choose carefully a few markets and to dominate them.

A key factor in competitive strategy is a bank's position against its competitors. This positioning determines whether a bank's profitability is above the industry average. Competitive positioning is often more important than the potential of the market. A bank that is well positioned can earn high rates of return even though the average profitability of the market is low. So what are the position choices open to banks?

Some banks aim to compete by positioning themselves as the lowest cost producer. Typically, they will sell standard, no-frills products and place great emphasis on price. If they can sell their services at the industry average price while their costs are below the industry average, they will make superior profits.

Other banks compete by being specialists. They select a market segment and tailor their strategy to serving it to the exclusion of all others. By focusing on target segments they can gain a competitive advantage over more broadly-based competitors, even though they have no competitive advantage in the banking business as a whole.

Yet other banks compete by differentiation. If we can be unique in our business in some way valued by buyers–in the product itself or in the delivery system through which it is sold–we can charge a premium for our services.

Often, banks persuade themselves that a middle course is most comfortable, less risky and adequately profitable. The evidence suggests that they are wrong. Few banks that have tried to do a little bit of everything have produced outstanding results. The likelihood is that tomorrow's great banks will be built on focus, not diversity and on markets, not products. Profits will come from finding new and better ways to serve our customers within our targeted markets, either as one of the few market leaders, who set the standard, or as a specialist, supplying a narrow range of products and services, but with such advantage in knowledge, service and adaptation to specific needs, as to be in a class on their own. An in-between position is rarely desirable or even viable over time. At best, it produces a middling performance.

This question of positioning has led many banks to re-examine their portfolio of businesses. Are we in the right mix of markets and products? Where should additional investments be made? Should we abandon certain activities? Should we diversify away from our present base? Should we change the character of our business?

These are major risk issues. There are no model answers. Each bank must reach its own decisions. But there are two basic principles that I would emphasise. First, in a fiercely competitive environment, the last thing we want to do is to spread our resources too thinly and with unnecessary risk over too wide an area. Second, we should be clear about how we are going to win in competition with others. A head-on, me-too approach will rarely be successful against entrenched competitors. In such cases, unless we can find new ways to serve customers, we should probably avoid the market.

This is a tough discipline to accept. The herd instinct among bankers is strong; all sorts of arguments are advanced for joining, or staying in; and those involved find it hard to be realistic about their competitive strengths. Yet bankers need to be able to say 'I will be in those three markets and products, but not in those two'. To attempt the impossible is not good strategy: it is just a waste of resources.

The profitability challenge

Declining profitability, measured by return on assets, remains probably the most serious single problem facing banks.

Banks have responded by using leverage to increase returns on equity to offset the effect of falling profit margins. Despite a declining return on assets, many banks have improved their return on equity by increasing leverage.

Leverage ratios for banks are usually based on comparisons of equity to total assets. What, in fact, is being measured is the amount by which assets exceed liabilities. The bigger the cushion, the greater the ability to withstand blows and still have enough assets to repay all liabilities. As leverage increases, this risk absorption ability declines. Two decades ago, the cushion was over 10 per cent of assets. In 1986, the average for the top 100 banks in the world was only 3.6 per cent.

As more attention has been focused on bank financial strength in general and bank capital ratios in particular, there has been a clear incentive for banks to avoid the appearance of increased leverage. So, banks have developed new products that generate income without generating assets. Such new products often involve different risk characteristics; in effect, equity capital has been leveraged further, even though the traditional leverage measurements may not have declined.

Obviously, constantly increasing leverage is an untenable policy: over time, risk assets – whether on the balance sheet or not – cannot continue to grow faster than equity; and there are now signs that banks have come to the end of that road. The introduction of new capital guidelines, on a risk adjusted basis, for US and UK banks, will require some banks to strengthen their capital ratios.

So volume growth alone is no longer a sufficient source of profit. Active management of the asset portfolio, changing the product mix, emphasising services that do not create risks and enhancing trading results will all require increased attention.

But what also has to be reversed is the deteriorating trend in the cost efficiency ratios of many banks. Unless this issue is tackled, those banks will be at a serious competitive disadvantage as high cost producers.

Although trimming costs can make a contribution to a cost reduction programme, the most effective way is to cut out some activities altogether. All too often plans concern themselves only with new and additional things to be done. Yet one of the most effective, and neglected, areas of improved performance is the systematic elimination of old activities which no longer make an important contribution.

The capital challenge

Over the next decade, banks will need large amounts of capital. First, extra capital will be needed to finance new product development, new technology, new equipment and new distribution networks. Second, capital will be required to finance growth. Third, additional capital will be necessary for those banks with an increasing involvement in capital markets activities. Fourth, more capital will be needed to strengthen capital ratios.

Yet, because of increased uncertainty and the risk of the new environment, the companies most in need of new equity tend to be those least able to acquire it at an acceptable cost.

Shareholders' expectations are rising. Along with increased competition for business, we are seeing increased competition for capital. Only those banks that are able to produce a return on equity in excess of their cost of equity and in excess of returns available from other investments will be those that meet investors' requirements.

There is a constant need to identify cash traps, i.e. businesses with permanent, negative cash flows that act as a drain on a bank's market value. Banks are loaded with cash traps, but they are usually buried in the larger businesses. If they can be eliminated, capital will be released for more profitable use elsewhere.

What all this reminds us is that, whatever the competition or the economic environment, our primary task is to manage our shareholders' funds as effectively and imaginatively as possible. The real question for the management of many financial institutions is: what collection of divestments, acquisitions and reallocations of capital is necessary to change our return on equity, market value, access to capital and ability to sustain appropriate growth? If we take this action, there is no shortage of capital for banks. But after years of easier options, these will be difficult decisions.

The technology challenge

Among the most profitable banking organisations in the years ahead will be those capable of delivering products and services at the lowest effective cost. To become low-cost producers, banks must plan the various elements of electronic banking in an integrated fashion. Few banks have yet succeeded in achieving this aim.

Systems and telecommunications have now become essential components in virtually all lines of business in banking. During the past decade, the proportion of technology expense to total operating expense has more than doubled and it is likely to account for an even higher proportion over the next decade.

What should the objectives be in using these techniques? The essential role and mission of the technology function is to ensure that our computer applications provide sufficient added value to the business. This leads us to the need to deliver improved productivity and a profitable increase in market share. Banks also add value to their services by creating benefits of these kinds in the hands of customers.

First, we can use technology as part of the long-term attack on our costs or on our customers' costs, as both profits and market share can be increased if a business can drive these operating costs down. For example, Lloyds Bank has successfully used computers in the UK in the past decade in this way in batch and on-line transaction processing.

Second, innovative uses of technology can help to focus product marketing on target customer groups and ensure that products are differentiated from those offered by the competition, so as to provide salesmen with a unique selling advantage. In the financial services industry there is limited product protection, but a well designed computer system can provide the necessary lead time for the product to become established and for it to become a market leader.

In product design, bank marketers should be aiming to provide unique selling opportunities based on systems that lock customers into products that save them money, or offer a unique quality or level of service, or provide particular added value in the information content of the service itself. Examples of each of these in turn include the corporate cash management terminal, the electronic cash dispenser, and retail asset management and company cash management services.

Third, technology can be used to access target markets through the traditional branch network and by other means.

In the personal market, one of the best examples has been the use of cash dispenser services, which have demonstrated remarkable growth in terms of numbers of cardholders, machines, variety of locations and transactions over the past ten years in particular. Customers have taken to them because they provide a quicker and more convenient way to withdraw cash, which remains the most popular method of retail payment.

In the commercial market, the introduction of technology-based cash management services has enabled banks to deliver information direct to the corporate treasurer through an office terminal, whilst the smaller businessman has his needs looked after by the invention of office banking packages. Information about the bank's own business and that of its customers will become more readily available as a means of managing the assets of both parties much more effectively. In future, we can expect to see this type of service enhanced so that our computers will be connected directly to the customers' machines in a variety of ways to extend the scope of the service.

In the 1990s, differences among banks' abilities to manage technology will become clearer and systems ability will become a significant barrier to entry into the financial services market. Superior technology is an element where genuine, sustainable, competitive advantage can be secured. Dramatic cost reductions are possible, which can transform a company's competitive position and sometimes completely change the basis of competition. There is little doubt that technology will be a key factor in determining the winners in years ahead.

The people challenge

Most financial institutions in the new, deregulated era face a major task of organisational readjustment. In ideal circumstances, this might be spread over a number of years. But the pace of competitor initiatives now dictates that time is short. So, developing an effective approach to organisational change is not an academic exercise. It is an urgent priority.

The toughest challenge and the most important step facing most banks is to build a more market-driven culture. I believe the magnitude of this shift in approach is not yet fully recognised. Ultimately, it means a change in the way we do business.

The culture, which is frequently present in large banks that have been relatively sheltered, through regulation, from the full rigour of market competition, tends to stress correct form and procedure in every activity. Quality control is based on the principle of rule books and inspections. Limited feedback is provided to staff. The organisation structure is typically hierarchical—with long chains of command. The result, inevitably, is a powerful incentive to avoid mistakes which tends to discourage risk taking and experimentation. The problem is that such a culture, while suited to a protected, regulated era, becomes exposed and vulnerable when competition intensifies.

Few would deny that a vital area in all of this is training. Training is seen as a good thing. But this is too general. The fact that one bank spends six per cent of its profit on training does not mean that it is a better bank than one that spends three per cent. The key test is the effectiveness of training in achieving the bank's objectives.

Can we agree on three important assumptions about training?

1. That the purpose of training is to change behaviour so that the person trained can perform a more effective and valuable service for the company.
2. That the effectiveness of training must be identifiable.
3. That the cost of training must be known in advance, be judged as tolerable by the employer, and controlled on a continuing basis.

So, it is essential to have people who are skilled in the fields of:
– Identification of training needs
– Specification of behavioural objectives
– Selection of training methods
– Administration of training programmes
– Appraising the value obtained from training.

It is also essential to require the business units to share the cost of training in proportion to their use. This has two advantages. The training group knows that it must produce a product that is seen by the buyer as cheaper, better or unique – because the business unit must be free to buy from the outside. For the buyer this approach requires more careful planning and budgeting. It also produces a more rational view of training and increased managerial involvement. It helps us to see training as a business investment with a clearly identifiable pay off.

With increased competition and the need for revitalisation, the focus of senior executive training and development programmes should be on corporate strategy and how to achieve it. With a practical and bottom-line focus, these programmes should be directing managers to analyse the company's competitive position and to come up with real action plans to achieve strategic goals.

Managers are going to have to think of themselves more as business managers and less as bankers.

The impetus for a successful, effective executive training and development programme comes from the very top of the organisation. The objectives must be clearly defined. The most important emphasis must be on the executive's role in implementing strategies and achieving goals. The top management team must be involved in the design of the programme. Top executives must be involved in the course itself. Each programme must be custom designed.

What all this means for our people is massive change. It will make our organisations less comfortable – and certainly less predictable – places to work in. It will create great uncertainty and few things can paralyse an organisation more than uncertainty.

One of the main tasks of top management, by words and actions, will be to reinforce the company's objectives, strategy and value system. It is essential for the whole team to know and be committed to where we want to go and how we are going to get there. It is an unending task. But without such leadership, there is little chance of sustained, superior performance in a rapidly changing environment.

Managing today's bank is a blend of strategy and action. Strategy and action must be developed together. Analysing options and allocating resources are not enough: management education, major changes in corporate beliefs and significant changes in real performance are what really matter.

So, what style of management is appropriate for today? The days of the autocrat seem over and so do those of the paternalist 'work hard, be a good boy and we'll look after you' regime. In the past, employees in many parts of the world have been somewhat fear motivated and security rewarded: they were willing to perform clerical, repetitive jobs and submit to autocratic hierarchies. In the future, they will demand changing tasks and greater participation.

In a complex and shifting world, leadership depends on trust and sharing organisational power, rather than operating through the more traditional top-down hierarchy.

Participative leadership rests on the conviction that managers, once they are deeply convinced of the need for change, will generate better solutions from their own commitment, experience and creativity. Above all, they will make them work.

We cannot change behaviour simply by issuing instructions. We can only change behaviour, and therefore strategy, by changing beliefs.

Change requires:

- Good, solid logic to justify the change
- Real commitment, forged through sharing in the development of the logic and the creation of new beliefs, strategies and actions
- Continued support, with new performance goals, incentives consistent with these goals, information flows which fit the new strategy and an organisational structure that helps to make the strategy happen.

The more the leader involves his team, the easier and better the change process, and the more likely that change will be continuous and productive. Success depends on people who understand and support the logic and then find ways to make it work, rather than back off or compromise as problems inevitably arise.

Conclusion

Banking is going through the kind of upheaval that industry has already faced. Today's competitive environment is tough, but it is going to get a lot tougher.

Top management is faced with the twin challenges of managing the basics of the business, particularly profitability and balance sheet strength, and, at the same time, restructuring the business to manage the sea change in the market.

All sorts of arguments will be advanced against radical action. Taking a long view is often a comfortable way of avoiding immediate and painful decisions. Others will argue that we must rush into new businesses otherwise we shall miss the bus. But new opportunities constantly arise and it is almost always possible to buy one's way back so long as the market value of your shares is strong. The key lies more in a superior market to book value than jumping in after more opportunity.

Success in business is a combination of caution and boldness: it requires both planning and courage. We shall need both to deal with the management challenges of the next few years. In George Orwell's words, the dilemma we face is this: 'The tendency is to make your environment safe and soft; and yet you are striving to keep yourself both brave and hard.'

I believe that we can pick ourselves through that dilemma, but only if we face up now to the reality of the competitive storms that lie ahead.

CASE STUDY

Corporate acquisition –
banker/customer relationships

DELTA FURNISHING GROUP

Introduction and History

Delta Furnishing Group is one of the oldest furniture businesses in the United Kingdom and has long been renowned for the superior quality and craftsmanship of its products. Originally, it was a family owned company, operating at the medium to upper end of the home furnishings market, designing and manufacturing its own furniture. For the last 20 years, however, Delta has operated solely as a retailer.

Trading difficulties were experienced in the early 1970s and, following modest expansion, a rescue operation was undertaken in 1980 by Davos PLC which acquired 80% of the share capital and funded working capital requirements. The balance of the shares was held by the directors.

Fortunes fluctuated through to September 1985, when a disastrous loss of £2.587 million was reported for the previous 18 month period. A new management team with proven retailing experience was brought in and, for the period to 30 September 1986, a major turnaround was achieved, producing a pre-tax profit of £4.07 million.

During the year, Davos decided to dispose of its 80% holding. This was taken out in October 1986 by a number of institutional investors. At the same time, some £18.7 million of cash was raised to repay amounts due to Davos and to provide additional working capital.

By October 1986 Delta had 75 High Street stores in the UK; 13 specialist Deltaplan stores in the UK and Europe; and 9 stores in the United States. The 75 UK furnishing stores were typically situated in prime locations with an average size of approximately 10,000 sq. ft.

Current Position

By December 1986 Delta's aggressive management decided to make a substantial acquisition. In January 1987 it acquired Blades Furniture Group which comprised 43 High Street stores and a further 10 edge-of-town stores (trading as Mammoth Furniture Stores). As a result, total UK selling space increased to 1.7 million sq. ft. in 138 stores. The cost of £8.1 million was met partly by a rights issue with the balance by issue of loan notes and Delta Group ordinary and preference shares. The rights issue, which raised £5.7 million net of expenses, also provided additional working capital for the Group.

The Future

Research has shown that the company's customer base is concentrated in the upper age bands. One of the primary aims of the new management team, therefore, is to create a stylish image within the stores and a better mix of merchandise to appeal to younger people with high disposable incomes. Although the Group ceased to manufacture furniture some 20 years ago, the directors have decided to consider the purchase of a manufacturing unit.

They also intend to restructure the Group by divisions, as follows:

(i) *Delta*
75 UK High Street stores, refurbished to a new Delta corporate image and aimed at the medium to upper end of the volume furnishings range.

(ii) *Deltaplan*
13 specialist stores—10 in the UK and 3 in Europe—trading at the top level of the furnishings market and requiring specialist buying and merchandising for their 'leading edge' image.

(iii) *Blades*
43 UK High Street stores currently serving the middle range of the volume furnishings market. (Whilst initially these stores will trade under the Blades Furniture name, the directors plan to refurbish/rationalise them into the Delta network within 5 years or so.)

(iv) *Mammoth Furnishings*

10 edge-of-town stores, aimed at the medium to upper end of the volume furnishings market.

(v) *Delta USA*

9 stores located in prime shopping mall sites in New York State and Florida, selling high quality furniture and furnishings.

The performance of the USA operation has been disappointing and, bearing in mind the management resources which will be required in the immediate future to integrate the remaining divisions, the directors have decided to dispose of it at an early date. Discussions are taking place with a prospective buyer.

A Further Acquisition

The June 1987 board meeting discussed the possibility of acquiring a manufacturing unit. Bedroom furniture is a strong selling line and, as part of the attack on the younger persons market, the directors would prefer to design and manufacture some of their popular ranges.

Discussions have already taken place with Alpha Furnishings Ltd., a furniture retailing operation with 11 out-of-town stores plus a manufacturing unit producing volume veneered furniture at a factory based in Newcastle. Alpha, a small family-controlled company established in 1972, has been managed from the outset by Robert Nicholson, who currently holds the position of Managing Director. A strong marketeer with rather less financial acumen, he has dominated boardroom discussions and overtrading has been the hallmark of the business. Turnover increased from £9.7 million in 1986 to £17.8 million in 1987. Although margins have been squeezed, Alpha achieved profits before tax of £0.716 million in 1986 and £1.452 million in 1987. Since incorporation, Alpha has banked with the Newcastle branch of Provincial Bank PLC, whose Head Office is in Nottingham. The relationship between the directors and the bank, both at branch and head office level, has always been good.

Alpha has been advised by an independent merchant bank on the

ways it might develop in future. Two strategies have been suggested:
  (i) to offer itself for takeover with retention contracts for key staff; or
  (ii) to strengthen the management team and seek a placing on the USM.

Recent balance sheets would support this course of action.

Delta Group, whose bankers are Federal Enterprise Bank PLC, is being advised by that bank's merchant banking arm. Whilst recognising that it needs the expertise of Alpha's key employees, Delta is concerned at merging the different cultures of the two companies.

Banking Requirements

The enlarged Delta/Alpha Furnishings Group will require the full range of banking services described in Appendix 1.

QUESTIONS

From the points of view of *both* banks concerned, and with regard to the requirements of the enlarged Delta Group and its proposed acquisition of Alpha Furnishings:
  1. What is the present status of the banking relationships with Delta Furnishing Group PLC and Alpha Furnishings Ltd?
  2. Where should the banks aim to be positioned following the acquisition?
  3. How should they set about achieving these positions?

N.B. The appendices to this case study give financial data for Delta Group and Alpha Furnishings, together with details of the key personnel in both companies. Information is also provided on the organisational structures of Federal Enterprise Bank and Provincial Bank.

APPENDIX 1

ISSUES TO BE ADDRESSED FROM THE VIEWPOINTS OF FEDERAL ENTERPRISE BANK PLC AND PROVINCIAL BANK PLC

(a) Analysis of the following:
Strengths
Weaknesses
Opportunities
Threats
considering, inter alia, the geography, product profile and organisational structure of each bank together with the corporate cultures of Delta Furnishing Group PLC and Alpha Furnishings Ltd.

(b) Identification and consideration of:
(i) Objectives – being measurable medium-term aims.
(ii) Appropriate strategies – how products will be exploited and resources mobilised to achieve objectives.
(iii) Goals – aspects of strategy to be achieved in the short-term.

(c) A review of the existing relationships (including profitability and contribution) together with an analysis of the competition and an evaluation of the related products and resources required in order to achieve the goals and objectives.

(d) Development of appropriate strategies and an implementation programme together with contingencies.

(e) Assessment of the importance of various banking services, principally:
Money transmission and clearing services.
Treasury management.
Electronic banking services.
Banking facilities short- and medium-term.

Together with:
H.P. and consumer credit finance.

Foreign exchange and international payments.
Guarantees.
Capital markets.
Company registrar services.
International services.
Banking for employees.
Pay services.
Relocation.
Insurance.
M & A advice.
Pension fund management.

APPENDIX 2

FEDERAL ENTERPRISE BANK PLC
PUBLIC COMPANY ACCOUNT SERVICING

As in all the major clearers, attention has been focused in recent years on specific market segments and products. The attached organisation chart (Appendix 2a) represents a typical structure with five business units. Three are basically 'customer segment driven' and the remainder 'product focused'.

Within this organisation, the major corporate sector is catered for by Corporate Division ('CD') chiefly taking care of companies with a net worth of £30 million plus. Smaller corporate relationships are handled within Retail Division ('RD').

Role & Function
CD's primary role is to:
−act as the focal point for the bank's relationship with major UK customers;
−co-ordinate relationships of the bank's overseas branches with the subsidiaries of UK companies.

Each customer group is allocated an account manager who, with a small team, is responsible for cultivating the relationship. Customer groups are handled on an industry sector basis (Appendix 2b).

Close relationships exist between CD managers and their counterparts in International Division ('ID'), Treasury Division ('TD') and the merchant bank, whose specialist knowledge can assist CD in its principal role of business development and the furtherance of corporate relationships.

(Appendix 2c sets out a typical matrix of relationships between the bank and ABC Group co-ordinated by CD in the centre.)

Business Objectives
Although the principal objective of CD (UK based) is to maintain and increase the volume of clearing business passing through its customers' current accounts, at the same time it aims to develop profitable, broadly based relationships with its customers in the provision of a wide range of banking services.

In the development of this market, CD benefits from the quality of its account managers, who provide a single point of contact with the bank as a whole. Each group of accounts is also allocated to a member of the general management team. This combination of account managers and the ultimate decision maker enables a speedy response to be given to customers' proposals – a major strength in the marketplace (Appendix 2d).

Products and Services
CD co-ordinates the delivery of banking services for its customers in the following areas:
–commercial – loans, deposits;
–electronic banking products;
–non funds-based income services;
–merchant banking products;
–treasury services.

These products and services are provided both within the UK and through overseas subsidiaries, circuits and branches.

APPENDIX 2a

FEDERAL ENTERPRISE BANK PLC — ORGANISATION CHART

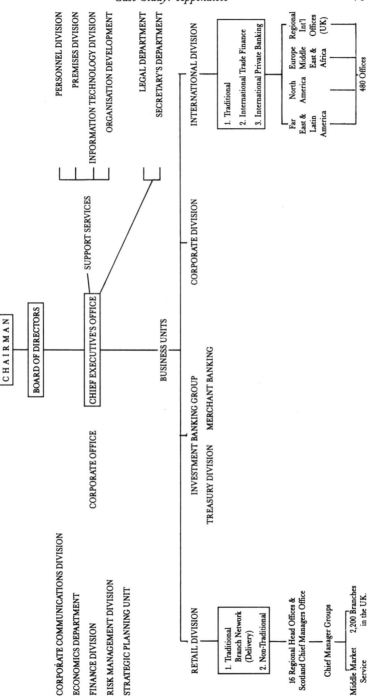

CHAIRMAN

BOARD OF DIRECTORS

CHIEF EXECUTIVE'S OFFICE

CORPORATE OFFICE

SUPPORT SERVICES

- PERSONNEL DIVISION
- PREMISES DIVISION
- INFORMATION TECHNOLOGY DIVISION
- ORGANISATION DEVELOPMENT
- LEGAL DEPARTMENT
- SECRETARY'S DEPARTMENT

- CORPORATE COMMUNICATIONS DIVISION
- ECONOMICS DEPARTMENT
- FINANCE DIVISION
- RISK MANAGEMENT DIVISION
- STRATEGIC PLANNING UNIT

BUSINESS UNITS

RETAIL DIVISION

1. Traditional Branch Network (Delivery)
2. Non-Traditional

16 Regional Head Offices & Scotland Chief Managers Office

Chief Manager Groups

Middle Market Service

2,200 Branches in the UK.

INVESTMENT BANKING GROUP

TREASURY DIVISION   MERCHANT BANKING

CORPORATE DIVISION

INTERNATIONAL DIVISION

1. Traditional
2. International Trade Finance
3. International Private Banking

Far East & Latin America

North America

Europe Middle East & Africa

Regional Int'l Offices (UK)

480 Offices

APPENDIX 2b

FEDERAL ENTERPRISE BANK PLC
INDUSTRY SECTORS

Asian Marketing
Automotive
Retailing and Breweries
Property and Building Products
Commodity Traders/Mining/Minerals
Conglomerates
Consumer Products
Electronics
Energy/Chemicals
Engineering/Conglomerates
Financial Services
Food Manufacture
Food/Minerals/Conglomerates
Gas/Plastics
General and Mechanical Engineering
Hotels/Property
Insurance
International Construction
Manufacturing/Engineering
Paper/Packaging/Publishing
Pharmaceuticals/Health Care
Public Utilities/Process Engineering
Transportation/Leisure

APPENDIX 2c **MARKETING INTERFACE WITH ABC GROUP**

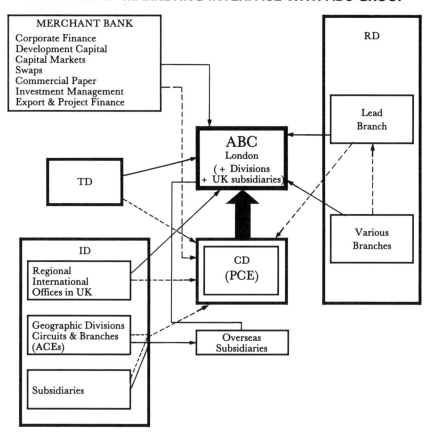

KEY:

⟶ denotes direct line of communication (from Federal Enterprise Bank Plc to ABC Group and vice versa)

- - - - - denotes internal communication within Federal Enterprise Bank Plc (from ACE to PCE and vice versa)

PCE — Parent Company Executive
ACE — Associate Company Executive

APPENDIX 2d
FEDERAL ENTERPRISE BANK PLC—CORPORATE DIVISION

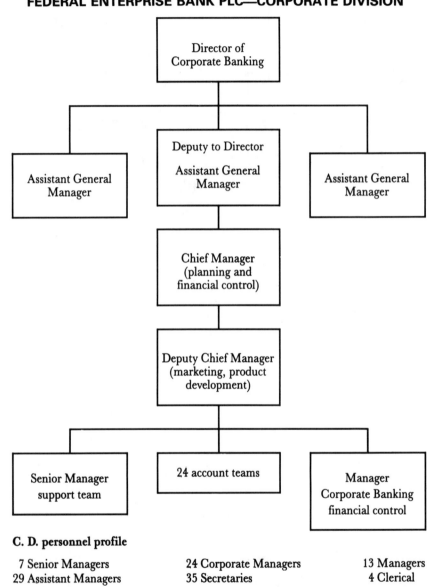

C. D. personnel profile

| 7 Senior Managers | 24 Corporate Managers | 13 Managers |
| 29 Assistant Managers | 35 Secretaries | 4 Clerical |

APPENDIX 3

PROVINCIAL BANK PLC—ORGANISATION STRUCTURE

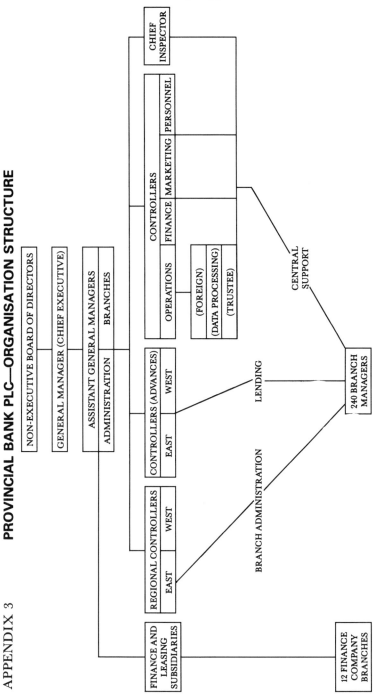

N.B. — The Bank's 240 branches are administered centrally from Head Office in Nottingham.

APPENDIX 4

Banking Relationships
(a) Delta Furnishing Group

Responsibility for the overall relationship rests with Federal Enterprise Bank's Corporate Division, although the bank accounts and borrowing facilities are domiciled at Federal's Oxford Street branch in London. The bank accounts of Blades are maintained at the Reading branch of the bank. In both cases, extensive use is made of the branch network for money transmission services.

Responsibility for the relationship lies with a 44 .year old Corporate Manager, who has only recently joined the Division after a two year attachment in Personnel in charge of graduate recruitment. Despite Federal's policy of attempting to maintain continuity between its managers and customers, this is the third Corporate Manager to handle the Delta account in the last two years.

The Oxford Street Branch Manager (aged 52) knew the Chairman and Group Chief Executive of Delta for many years before they joined the board in 1985. He was instrumental in negotiating a revised financing package in that year, shortly before overall responsibility for the connection was transferred to Corporate Division who by then had spotted the Group's growth potential.

Remuneration Summary – Half Year to June 1987

Money Transfer Services		– Cost	£137,323
		– Revenue	£131,818
			(£5,505)
Lending Services			
Cost of Control	£3,000		
Cost of Funds	£513,707		
		– Cost	£516,707
Interest Received	£520,250		
Lending Fees	£1,000		
		– Revenue	£521,250
			Profit £4,543

Banking Facilities

Parent Company

Overdraft and/or Acceptance Credits	£10 million
Committed Money Market Line	£3 million
(multi-currency)	
Five year Medium-Term Loan	£2.5 million
Loan Note Guarantee	£2.75 million
BACS	£1 million

Blades

Overdraft	£4 million
Three year Medium-Term Loan	£1.5 million
Customs & Excise Guarantees	£0.25 million
BACS	£0.15 million

Security

All borrowing facilities are secured by first charges over the Group's freehold and leasehold property interests.

Pricing

Overdraft	1¾% above base rate
Acceptance Credits	½% on face value of bill
Committed Money Market Line	1½% above cost of funds
Medium-Term loans	1⅛% above LIBOR inclusive
Loan Note Guarantee	¾% per annum
Customs & Excise Guarantees	½% per annum

(b) Alpha Furnishings

Day to day administration of the account is in the hands of the Manager and Assistant Manager of Provincial's Newcastle branch, both of whom have a good working relationship with the company's Financial Director.

Senior officials from Advances Control Division at Head Office enter into any discussions on lending facilities afforded to the company. The branch officials also join in these meetings, which usually involve both the Managing Director and Financial Director of Alpha. The continuing close involvement of the central advances officials results in a speedy response to any request from the company for revised facilities.

Debit Interest
1½ per cent over base on trading account
2 per cent over base on loan account
The loan account is repayable by monthly instalments over ten years.

Commission
£0.09 per cent on debit turnover, yielding 30 per cent profit to the bank. Total income, including charges for ancillary services, is approximately £30,000 per annum.

Security
Debenture giving fixed and floating charges over all the company's assets.

APPENDIX 5

MAIN PERSONALITIES INVOLVED

(a) Delta Furnishing Group – London

Chairman John Dobson – Age 60
Joined the board early in 1985. Has spent over 40 years in retailing and was Chairman of a highly successful electrical retailers until its takeover by an American company in 1983.

Group Chief Executive: Richard Ridgeway – Age 40
Joined the board at the same time as the Chairman. Spent 15 years in retailing and was himself a casualty of a takeover bid in 1984, when he lost his position as Managing Director of an automotive products retailer.

Finance Director: Julian Critchley – Age 54
Background in accountancy and financial institutions. Finds it difficult to fit into the close-knit management team bearing in mind his lack of retail experience. It is likely that he will be replaced before long.

The remainder of the board are all experienced retailers – Reginald Godstone is Group Merchandise Director; Peter White, Group Operations Director; Larry Johnson, Group Sales and Marketing Director; and Malcolm Gray is Group Personnel Director.

Reporting to the main board directors are 10 associate directors, all of whom have been with the company less than 3 years. There are 19 executives at the next level of management who fulfil line and specialist positions within the organisation.

The firm's recent policy has been to recruit experienced people at both regional and store management levels and the directors believe that the key positions are now all filled by people of the necessary calibre. Considerable emphasis is placed upon training, including customer service skills and product knowledge courses.

(b) Alpha Furnishings – Newcastle upon Tyne

Managing Director: Robert Nicholson – Age 50
Founder of the business fifteen years ago with father and a brother, both of whom have now left the company.

A forceful personality. Main strength lies in his ability to detect opportunities to open new, profitable outlets for the business. Very much marketing minded but less strong on the financial side of the business. Until recently his marketing drive overshadowed the personalities involved in financial control and so overtrading has been the hallmark of the business.

Commercial Director: Derek Wilson – Age 42
Until recently Financial Director, a position he had held for several years.

A competent man but lacking the strength of character required to balance the dominating marketing stance taken by the Managing Director. Has now assumed responsibility for the development of computer-based management information systems.

Financial Director: Martin Buchanan – Age 38
Recently appointed from outside the company in recognition of the earlier weaknesses in financial control. Too early to say whether the appointment will bring the desired strengthening of the financial side of the management structure.

Sales Director: Brian Thomas – Age 41
Appointed recently to support the Managing Director who had previously given himself sole responsibility for sales. Thomas is rapidly consolidating his position and should be capable of shouldering the burden of meeting the Managing Director's appetite for growth.

Administration Director: William Cross – Age 37
Another recent appointment. Responsibilities include personnel matters, stock control and branch administration, including premises acquisition and layout.

Operations Director: Norman Vincent – Age 58

Has come up through the ranks on the production side of the company. Lack of financial skills has not been exposed as the manufacturing operation has never been run as a separate profit centre.

APPENDIX 6

DELTA FURNISHING GROUP PLC

CONSOLIDATED PROFIT AND LOSS ACCOUNT
For the year ended 30 September 1986

	1986 £000	18 months ended 30 September 1985 £000
Turnover	99,333	152,712
Cost of sales	(64,285)	(100,122)
Gross profit	35,048	52,590
Selling and distribution costs	(29,194)	(48,856)
Administration expenses	(5,973)	(11,323)
Other operating income	3,909	4,488
Operating profit/(loss)	3,790	(3,101)
Interest receivable	150	299
Interest payable	(1,328)	(2,397)
Surplus on property disposals	1,458	2,612
Profit/(loss) on ordinary activities before taxation	4,070	(2,587)
Taxation (charge)/credit	(245)	520
Profit/(loss) on ordinary activities after taxation	3,825	(2,067)
Extraordinary items	—	(5,599)
Profit/(loss) after extraordinary items	3,825	(7,666)
Dividends paid and proposed	—	(117)
Retained profit/(loss) for the year	3,825	(7,783)

DELTA FURNISHING GROUP PLC

BALANCE SHEET
30 September 1986

	1986 £000	*Group*	1985 £000
Fixed assets			
Tangible assets	33,807		31,711
Investments in subsidiary companies	—		—
	33,807		31,711
Current assets			
Stocks	17,688		17,268
Debtors	10,971		6,302
Short-term loan	—		8,500
Cash at bank and in hand	3,589		1,208
	32,248		33,278
Creditors (amounts falling due within one year)	(33,631)		(38,262)
Net current (liabilities)/assets	(1,383)		(4,984)
Total assets less current liabilities	32,424		26,727
Creditors (amounts falling due after more than one year)	(2,584)		(1,623)
Provisions for liabilities and charges	(550)		(505)
	29,290		24,599
Capital and reserves			
Called up share capital	3,899		3,899
Share premium account	232		232
Revaluation reserve	12,810		12,441
Profit and loss account	12,349		8,027
	29,290		24,599

APPENDIX 7

ALPHA FURNISHINGS GROUP

Synopsis of present situation

The directors have recognised that the present capital base is inadequate to support the levels of activity seen.

The company is well down the road in negotiations with a merchant bank for a flotation of shares on the USM–scheduled for October 1987.

The flotation will involve the issue of new shares to raise a minimum of £2.25 million (net) for the company. The proceeds will be used to reduce debt by £1.5 million and to finance future store expansion. Two directors will also sell part of their shareholdings to raise substantial personal sums from the flotation. The Managing Director will retain a controlling interest.

The company intends to maintain its expansion programme by opening at least four outlets per year. On average the capital cost of a new store is £250,000.

The management of the company has been reinforced recently by the appointment of new Sales, Financial and Administration Directors. The Managing Director is now satisfied that the corporate structure meets the present and future needs of the company.

The store network reflects the recent corporate decision to rationalise operations in the traditional area (the North East) and seek to expand in the South of England, which has not been affected to the same degree by the general economic recession. All that remains of the original North East network are branches at Newcastle, Gateshead and Darlington.

Within the last eighteen months, stores have been opened at Guildford, Bristol, Swindon, Luton, Croydon, Potters Bar, Richmond and Peterborough.

ALPHA FURNISHINGS GROUP

GROUP PROFIT AND LOSS ACCOUNT
For the year ended 30 June 1987

	Note	1987 £000's	1986 £000's
TURNOVER		17,758	9,686
Cost of sales		10,397	5,052
GROSS PROFIT		7,361	4,634
Other operating expenses (net)		5,476	3,628
OPERATING PROFIT		1,885	1,006
Interest payable and similar charges	1	433	290
PROFIT ON ORDINARY ACTIVITIES BEFORE TAXATION	2	1,452	716
Taxation		450	238
PROFIT FOR THE FINANCIAL YEAR		1,002	478
Dividend		51	21
RETAINED PROFIT FOR THE YEAR		951	457

ALPHA FURNISHINGS GROUP

GROUP BALANCE SHEET
30 June 1987

	Note	1987 £000's	1986 £000's
FIXED ASSETS			
Tangible assets	4	3,841	2,315
Investments		—	1,093
		3,841	3,408
CURRENT ASSETS			
Stocks	5	4,408	2,665
Debtors	6	3,036	2,142
Cash at bank and in hand		112	196
		7,556	5,003
CREDITORS: Amounts falling due within one year	7	8,030	5,354
NET CURRENT LIABILITIES		(474)	(351)
TOTAL ASSETS LESS CURRENT LIABILITIES		3,367	3,057
CREDITORS: Amounts falling due after more than one year	8	(933)	(604)
PROVISION FOR LIABILITIES AND CHARGES		(531)	(551)
		1,903	1,902
CAPITAL AND RESERVES			
Called up share capital		1,001	992
Share premium account		212	—
Revaluation reserve		222	—
Profit and loss account		468	910
		1,903	1,902

Notes
1. INTEREST PAYABLE AND SIMILAR CHARGES:

	1987 £000's	1986 £000's
On bank loans, overdrafts and other loans —repayable within five years, by instalments	299	244
On finance leases and hire-purchase contracts	47	46
On all other loans	87	—
	433	290

2. PROFIT ON ORDINARY ACTIVITIES
   BEFORE TAXATION:
   Profit on ordinary activities before taxation
   is stated after charging (crediting)

	1987 £000's	1986 £000's
Staff costs (note 3)	2,462	1,628
Depreciation of tangible fixed assets	446	323
Loss on disposal of tangible fixed assets	112	—
Auditors' remuneration	40	36
Operating lease costs	364	171
Lease rentals receivable	(3)	(65)

3. STAFF COSTS:
   Employee costs during the year amounted to

	1987 £000's	1986 £000's
Wages and salaries	2,228	1,486
Social security costs	221	142
Other pension costs	13	—
	2,462	1,628

The average weekly number of persons employed
by the group during the year was as follows:

	1987	1986
Production, distribution and selling	182	157
Administration	89	82

4. SCHEDULE OF FIXED ASSETS
The movement in the year was as follows

| | Land and buildings | | | | Plant, equipment and motor vehicles £000's | Total £000's |
	Freehold £000's	Investment property £000's	Long leasehold £000's	Short leasehold £000's		
COST OR VALUATION						
Beginning of year	984	—	—	75	2,088	3,147
Additions	—	—	358	23	1,278	1,659
Disposals	—	—	—	(24)	(1,090)	(1,114)
New subsidiaries	—	240	—	264	328	832
Arising on revaluation	116	—	19	—	—	135
	1,100	240	377	338	2,604	4,659
DEPRECIATION						
Beginning of year	67	—	—	35	730	832
Charge	17	—	3	9	417	446
Disposals	—	—	—	(8)	(514)	(522)
New subsidiaries	—	—	—	52	97	149
Written back on revaluation	(84)	—	(3)	—	—	(87)
	—	—	—	88	730	818
NET BOOK VALUE (end of year)	1,100	240	377	250	1,874	3,841

Freehold land amounting to £120,000 at valuation and £39,000 at cost (1986—£39,000 at cost) is not depreciated.

The net book value of plant, equipment and motor vehicles held under finance lease agreements and hire-purchase contracts included above is £717,000 (1986—£490,000) and the related depreciation charge for the year is £85,000 (1986—£124,000).

5. STOCKS:

	1987 £000's	1986 £000's
Raw materials and consumables	1,917	2,099
Work in progress	56	86
Finished goods and goods for resale	2,435	480
	4,408	2,665

6. DEBTORS:

	1987 £000's	1986 £000's
Amounts falling due within one year		
Trade debtors	2,359	1,532
Other debtors	151	85
Prepayments and accrued income	420	50
Deferred showroom costs	106	139
	3,036	1,806
Amounts falling due after more than one year		
Trade debtors	—	336
	3,036	2,142

7. CREDITORS–AMOUNTS FALLING DUE WITHIN ONE YEAR:

	1987 £000's	1986 £000's
Bank loans (secured)	76	153
Bank overdraft (secured)	2,134	1,135
Payments received on account	354	235
Obligations under finance leases and hire-purchase contracts	326	212
Trade creditors	3,786	3,051
Other creditors:		
–UK corporation tax payable	470	86
–ACT	—	9
–VAT	188	148
–social security and PAYE	147	88
–other creditors	—	42
Accruals and deferred income	549	195
	8,030	5,354

The bank loans and overdrafts are secured by fixed and floating charges over the group's assets.

8. CREDITORS–AMOUNTS FALLING DUE
    AFTER MORE THAN ONE YEAR:

	1987 £000's	1986 £000's
Obligations under finance leases and hire-purchase contracts	221	57
Mortgage loan	164	—
Bank loans	548	547
	933	604

Analysis of bank loans:

	1987 £000's	1986 £000's
Secured loan repayable by monthly instalments of £5,500 commencing 11 March 1986 with interest at 2% above base rate (1986–repayable in annual instalments of £65,000)	458	547
Secured loan repayable by annual instalments of £10,000 maturing 30 November 1996 attracting variable interest rates	90	—
	548	547

Analysis of borrowing:

	1987 £000's	1986 £000's
Due within five years		
–within 1 year –bank	76	153
–leases	326	212
–within 1-2 years–bank	76	65
–leases	111	57
–within 2-5 years–bank	294	260
–leases	110	—
	993	747
Due wholly or in part by instalments over five years:		
–bank loans	178	222
Due otherwise than by instalments after five years:		
–mortgage loan	164	—
	1,335	969
Amounts due within one year (note 7)		
–bank loans	(76)	(153)
–leases	(326)	(212)
	933	604

DISCUSSION SYLLABUS 1

Focusing on the clearing banks*, an analysis of the present health of the industry – strengths, weaknesses, opportunities and likely threats (response to competition etc.).

Factors to be Considered

1. Defining the parameters of the industry of which the clearing banks form a part.
   (a) The *markets* in which the clearing banks are now operating and the *customers* which they are targeting retail, corporate, international, investment banking. (Note: the clearers' *retail* operations will be the subject of detailed analysis in Discussion Syllabus 2.)
   (b) The *participants* in these markets at home and abroad:
      i) at home – established banking participants (other domestic retail banks, accepting houses, foreign banks based in the UK, etc.) and new participants (e.g. building societies, large retailers, life assurance companies);
      ii) abroad – other international banks and securities houses, indigenous financial institutions.
   (c) The *products* and *services* provided in these markets:
      i) traditional banking services (money transmission, deposits, lending);
      ii) new products and services (investment banking, insurance, mortgages etc.).
2. It has been suggested that the clearing banks have operated comfortably within a monopolistic industry for far too long and that they will have to work harder in the future to maintain commensurate levels of profit growth.
   The strengths and weaknesses of the clearing banks in the newly defined industry regarding:
   (a) environmental issues (economic, financial, regulatory, technological);
   (b) financial robustness (capital, provisioning, profitability);
   (c) resources and organisation;
   (d) corporate life cycle;
   (e) competitor positioning;

(f) the customers;
(g) product range/mix.
Some key indicators of clearing bank performance over the last five years are set out in the appendix.
3. The enlarged industry undoubtedly creates both opportunities and threats for the clearing banks. From an appraisal of their strengths and weaknesses, conclusions should be drawn on:
   (a) the opportunities available to the clearing banks for maximising their business;
   (b) the major threats to the clearing banks, and how they can protect themselves against these threats.

QUESTIONS

1. What are the **adverse** forces currently at work in the market and influencing the clearing banks' profitability?
2. What are the **favourable** forces?
3. What are the various strategies – in terms of markets, customers, products, organisational structures etc. – adopted by the clearing banks to cope with these forces (both adverse and favourable)? And how are they currently placed?

*N.B. For the purposes of this syllabus the term "clearing banks" is used in the context of the 'Big Four' UK banks (Barclays, Lloyds, Midland and National Westminster).

STATISTICAL APPENDIX

The 'Big Four' Clearing Banks: 1982-86

		1982	1983	1984	1985	1986
1	Total assets (£bns)	190.3	208.9	243.8	239.6	263.3
	% change	+21.9%	+9.8%	+16.7%	-1.7%	+9.9%
2	Total equity (£bns)	9.4	10.6	9.6	10.7	13.4
	% change	+16.2%	+12.5%	-9.8%	+12.3%	+25.0%
3	Equity/assets ratio	4.9%	5.1%	3.9%	4.5%	5.1%
4	Free capital ratio	4.2%	4.8%	4.5%	6.5%	6.9%
5	Pre-tax profits (£mns)	1469	1647	1879	2556	3040
	% change	-10.6%	+12.1%	+14.1%	+36.0%	+18.9%
6	Post-tax profits (£mns)	1133	1087	788	1364	1971
	% change	-12.4%	-4.1%	-27.5%	+73.1%	+44.5%
7	Return on average assets (pre-tax)	0.84%	0.82%	0.81%	1.09%	1.21%
8	Return on average assets (post-tax)	0.65%	0.54%	0.34%	0.58%	0.78%
9	Return on average equity (pre-tax)	16.7%	16.6%	19.3%	25.4%	25.9%
10	Return on average equity (post tax)	12.8%	11.0%	8.1%	13.6%	16.8%
11	Net interest margins:					
	domestic	5.91%	5.46%	5.52%	5.58%	5.49%
	international	2.10%	2.13%	2.14%	2.11%	1.96%
	total	3.59%	3.40%	3.37%	3.56%	3.59%
12	Cost/income ratio	72%	71%	69%	67%	67%
13	Total bad debt charge (£mns)	972	1276	1761	1442	1361
	As a % of average loans to customers	0.91%	0.99%	1.16%	0.96%	0.87%
14	Total provisions outstanding (£mns)	2178	2997	3789	3916	4218
	As a % of loans to customers	1.82%	2.19%	2.34%	2.55%	2.60%

DISCUSSION SYLLABUS 2

The organisational implications in developing retail operations in a rapidly changing, competitive environment. The challenges ahead for the banks.

Introduction

Clear distinctions between the different types of financial institutions no longer exist. Many retailers offer financial services whereas banks offer services only remotely connected with banking. New technology means that the usefulness of branch networks is open to question. Change is essential, but is it the banker, the competitor or the customer who determines the pace of that change?

Aims of Discussion

1. Focusing on the retail aspects of Discussion Syllabus 1, to decide what business the UK clearing banks should be in.
2. To consider what type of retail network the public is likely to demand, and the ability of the banks to meet those needs.
3. To discuss the changing nature of delivery systems and the major impacts of technological advances.
4. To consider the effects upon management and staff of the expected changes. To what extent are staff issues a major factor in determining the pace of change?

Factors to be Considered

1. (a) Changing nature of the market place.
   (b) The erosion of traditional banking services.
   (c) The impact of new product packaging.
   (d) Differentiation between banking strategies.
   (e) Relative profitability of different services.

2. (a) Traditional banking networks – spread, costs, etc. The cost of change.
   (b) The spread of alternative retail approaches.
   (c) Customer acceptance of change – corporate and personal.
   (d) Customer service standards in a technological age.

3. (a) Technological developments and their impact to date.
  (b) Future technological innovations required by customers.
  (c) The decision-making process for technological investments.

4. (a) Changing management skills and structures.
  (b) Resource costs and planning implications.
  (c) Labour relations; the impact of specialisation.
  (d) Quality requirements, recruitment policies, early retirement policies.
  (e) Staff mobility – not only geographically but within and between organisations.
  (f) Reward systems.

QUESTIONS

1. How far is the speed of change in the methods of delivering banking services likely to be influenced by competitor activity; the demands of customers; and the banks' own positions in the market place?
2. Who should determine what technological investments are made: the banker; the technologist; or the customer? Why?
3. Human resources have to be managed more effectively than ever before. Banks have to match – successfully – their planning needs with a cost effective structure whilst maintaining the flexibility to meet the challenges of the developing market place. What problems do they face in seeking to re-educate and motivate their staff, and how might these be overcome?

READING LIST

This select reading list and the publications it refers to were circulated to members before the seminar. The publications were available for reference at Christ's College, Cambridge, during the seminar.

1. Managing the relationships with corporate customers, by Ian Watson. *International Journal of Bank Marketing*, vol. 4, no. 1, 1986.

2. Are non-banks winning in retail financial services?, by Philip Middleton. *International Journal of Bank Marketing*, vol. 5, no. 1, 1987.

3. Image in retail banking, by J. Barry Howcroft and John Lavis. *International Journal of Bank Marketing*, vol. 4, no. 4, 1986.

4. Can 'marketing' be made to work?, by Guy de Moubray. *The Banker*, May 1986.

5. Revamping the High Street image. *Banking World*, December 1986.

6. Bank strategies for the 1990s. Cambridge Seminar 1986. *The Institute of Bankers*, 1986.

7. Is this the age of the universal bank?, by Anthony Rohlwink. *The Banker*, January 1987.

8. Structural and organisational choices in an international bank, by Deryk Vander Weyer *in* Management and people in banking. 2nd Edn., ed. by Bryan L. Livy. *The Institute of Bankers*, 1985.

9. Banking Act 1979: *annual report by the Bank of England 1986–87.*

10. How Lloyds hopes to hone its edge, by Charles Leadbeater. *Financial Times*, 29 May 1987.

11. Strategic management of technology, by Trevor Nicholas *in* Competition and co-operation in world banking. *The Institute of Bankers*, 1985.

Cambridge Seminar
Programme

6–11 September 1987

Banking Through the Looking Glass

Sunday
6 September

20.30–20.45 Plenary briefing session

20.50–21.45 Informal discussion

Monday
7 September

THE PERSONAL
CUSTOMER'S VIEW

08.45–09.55 Discussion of paper and
preparation of questions

10.00–10.30 Introduction by Professor
DEREK CHANNON,
Professor of Marketing,
Manchester Business
School

11.00–12.30 Plenary Questions and
Answers

14.30–15.55 Discussion Syllabus 1

16.30–18.00 Discussion Syllabus 1
Plenary Session

20.30–21.30 Informal discussion

Tuesday
8 September

THE CORPORATE
CUSTOMER'S VIEW

08.45–09.55 Discussion of paper and
preparation of questions

10.00–10.30 Introduction by ROBERT
CARLTON-PORTER,
ACIB, Finance Director,
English China Clays Plc

11.00–12.30 Plenary Questions and
Answers

14.30–15.55 Case Study

14.30–15.55 Case Study

20.30–21.30 Presentation by The
Yellowhammer Advertising
Co. Ltd.

Wednesday
9 September

THE COMPETITOR'S
VIEW

08.45–09.55 Discussion of paper and
preparation of questions

10.00–10.30 Introduction by MARK
BOLEAT,
Director-General, The
Building Societies
Association

11.00–12.30 Plenary Questions and
Answers

14.30–15.55 Case Study
Plenary Session

16.30–18.00 Discussion Syllabus 2

20.30–21.30 Informal discussion

Thursday
10 September

A BANKER'S VIEW

08.45–09.55 Discussion of paper and
preparation of questions

100

Seminar Programme

10.00–10.30 Introduction by BRIAN
PITMAN, FCIB, Chief
Executive, Lloyds Bank Plc

11.00–12.30 Plenary Questions and
Answers

14.30–16.30 Discussion Syllabus 2
Plenary Session

18.45   Reception

19.30   Farewell Dinner

Friday
11 September

Depart

101

PREVIOUS CAMBRIDGE SEMINARS

Year	Theme	Director
1986	Bank Strategies for the 1990s*	George Walters
1984	Financing New Technology*	Don Fiddes, FCIB
1983	The Banks and Personal Customers*	Alan Miller, FCIB
1982	The Banks and Technology in the 1980s*	Eric Glover
1981	The Banks and the Public*	Peter Spiro
1980	The Banks and their Competitors*	Eric Glover
1978	The Banks and Small Businesses	George Walters
1977	Banks and the British Exporter	David Whelpton
1976	The Banks and Industry	Eric Glover
1975	The Branch Banker: Today and Tomorrow	Geoffrey Dix, OBE
1974	The Banks and Society	David Whelpton
1972	Banking for Profit	Eric Glover
1971	The Marketing of Bank Services	Geoffrey Dix, OBE
1969	Bank Management—Recruitment and Training	Henry Eason
1968	The Future of British Banking	Henry Eason

In those years where no Cambridge Seminar was held The Institute of Bankers was host to the International Banking Summer School. The papers and case studies from previous seminars marked with an asterisk above are still available from the Institute.